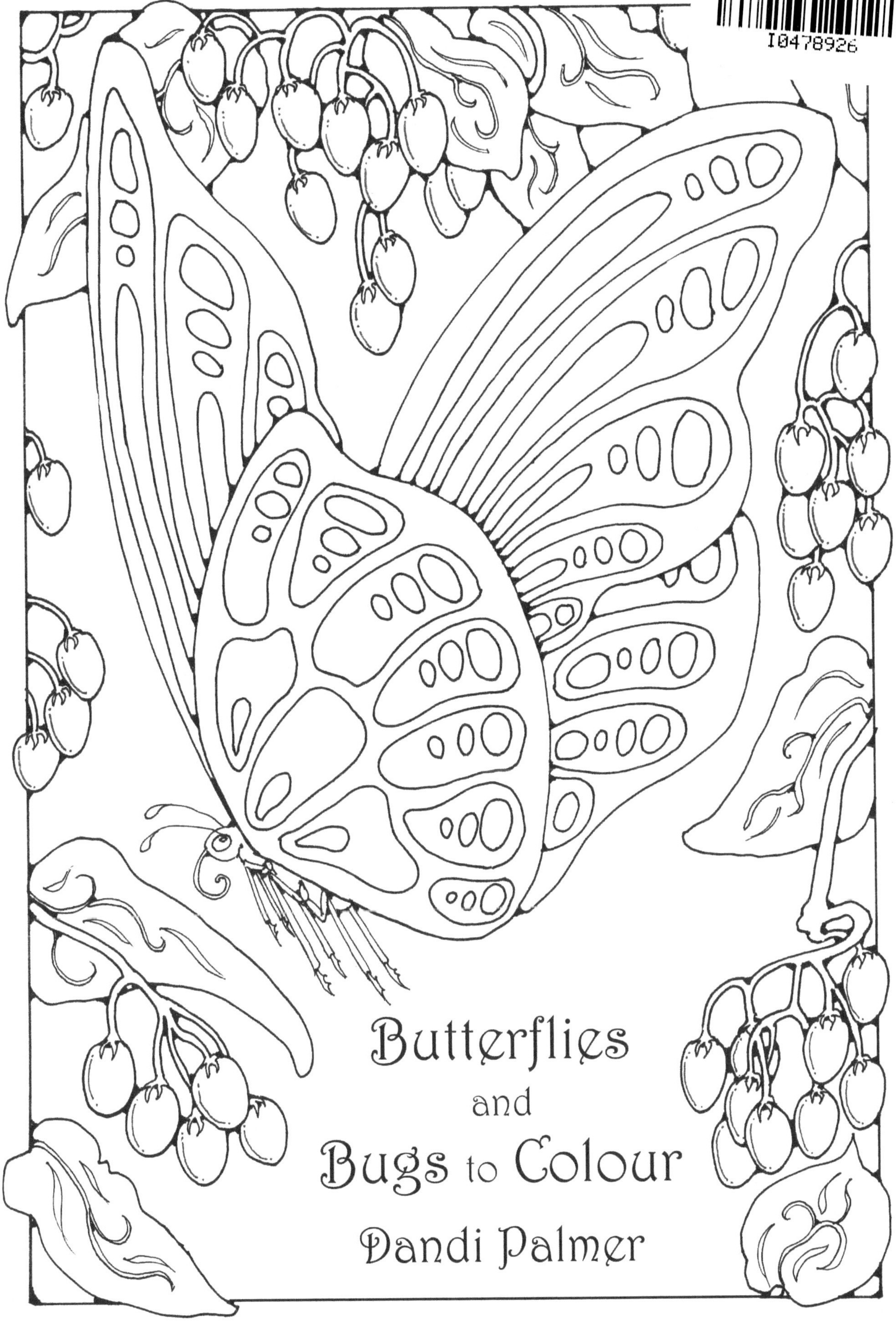

Butterflies and Bugs to Colour

Dandi Palmer

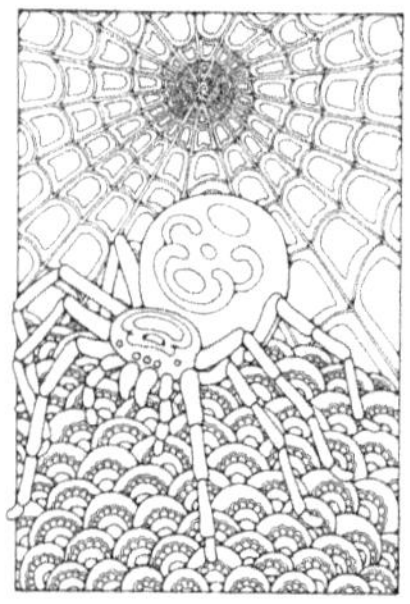
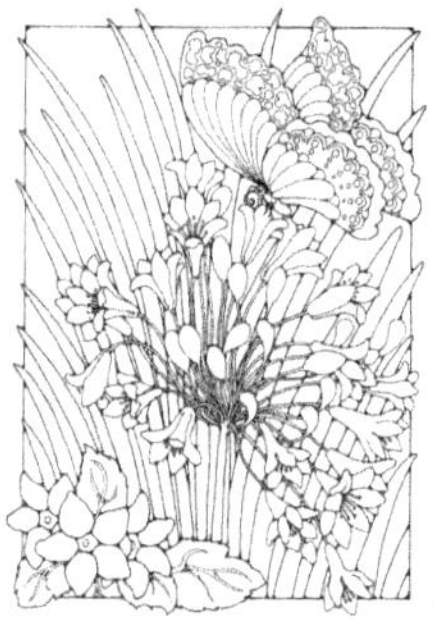
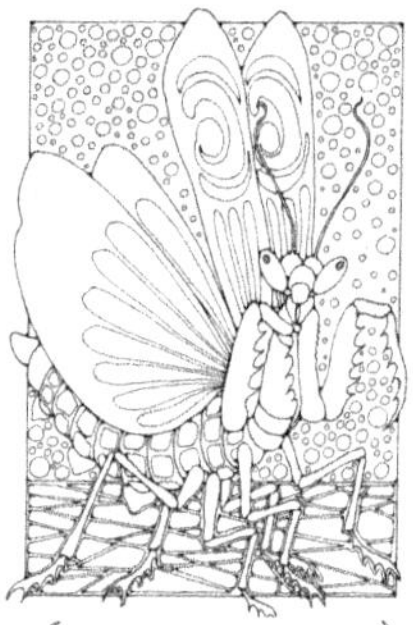
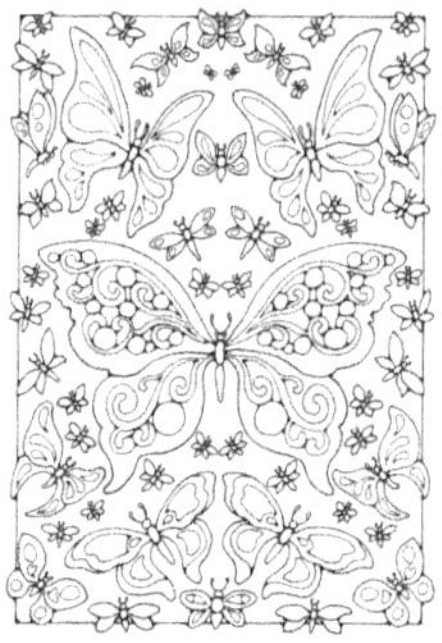
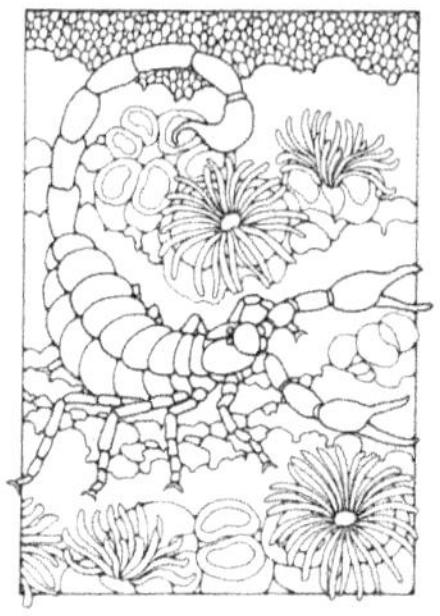
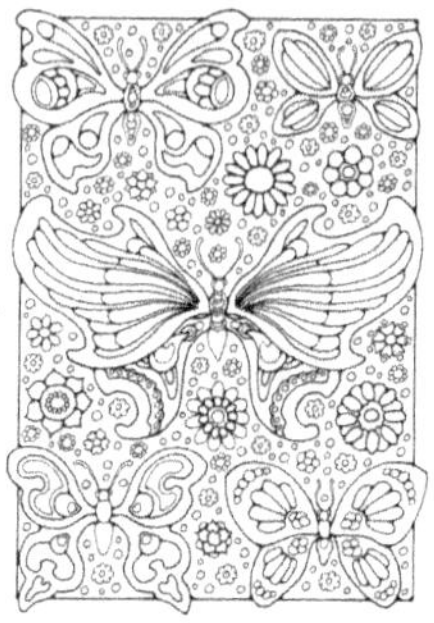
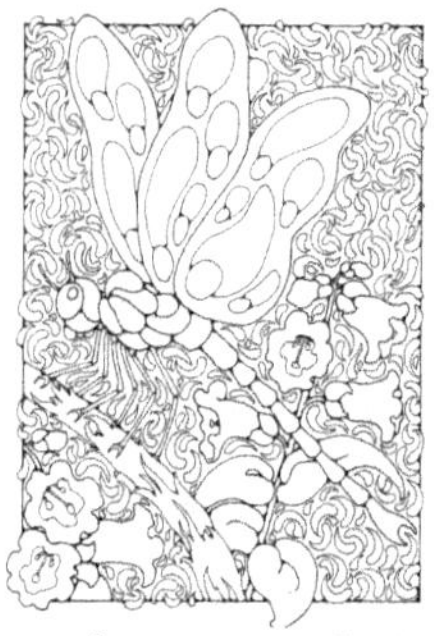
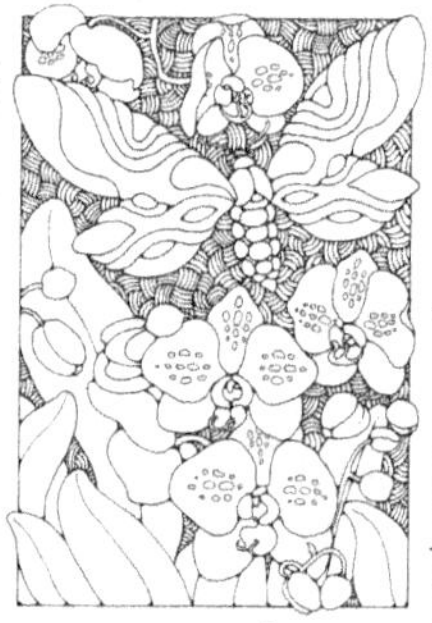
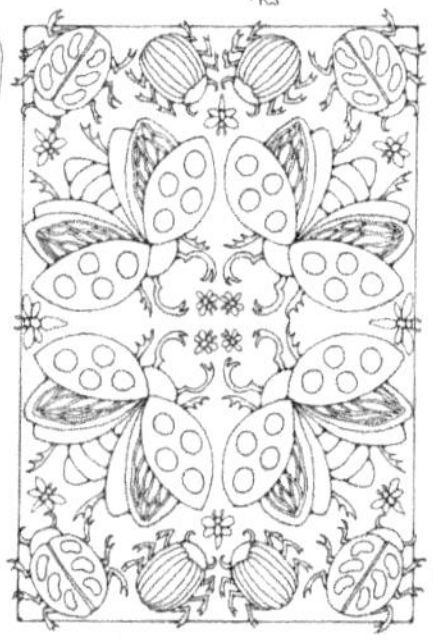
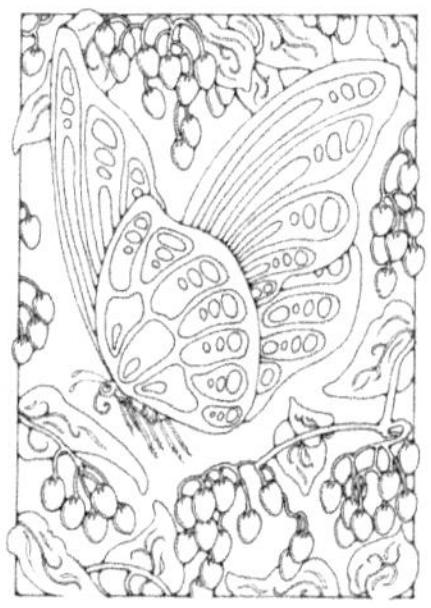
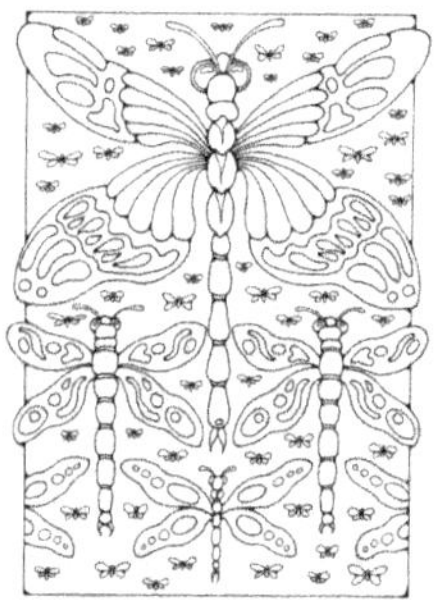
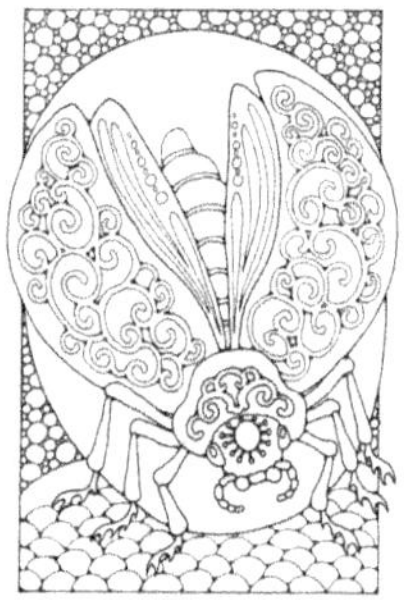
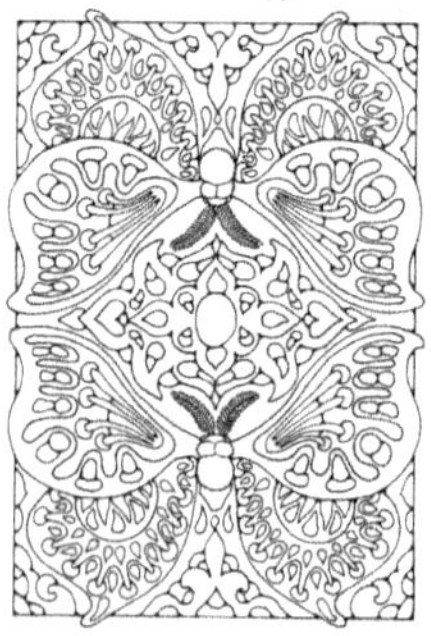
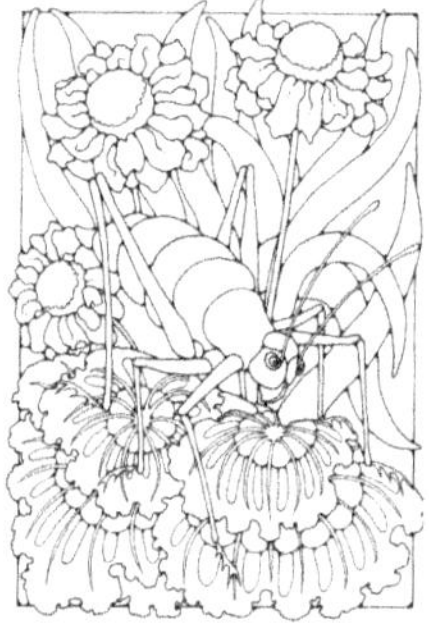
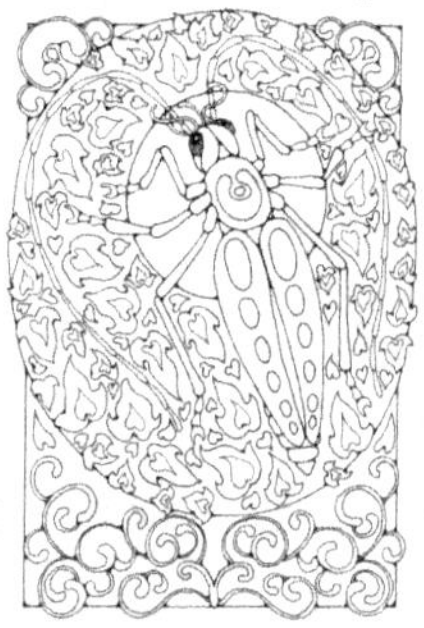
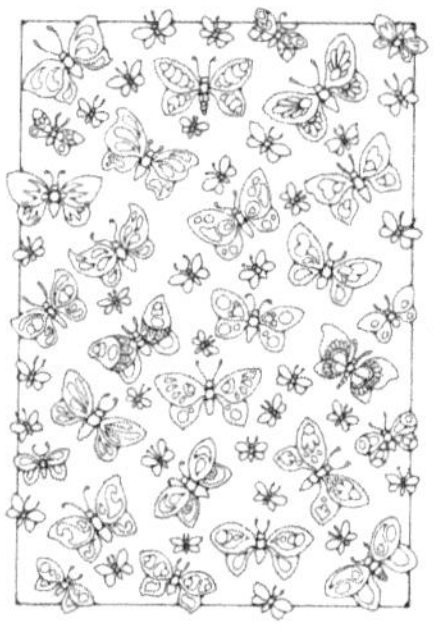
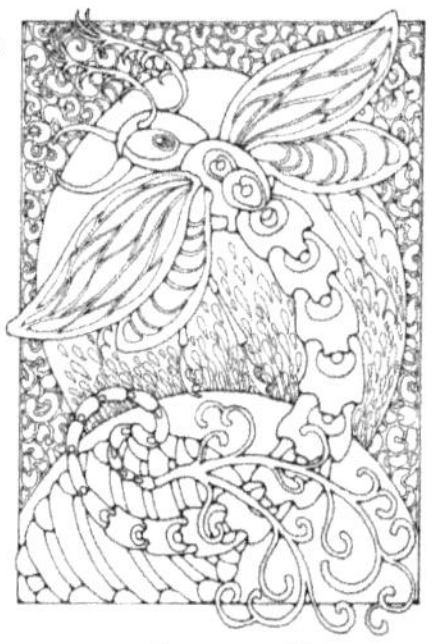
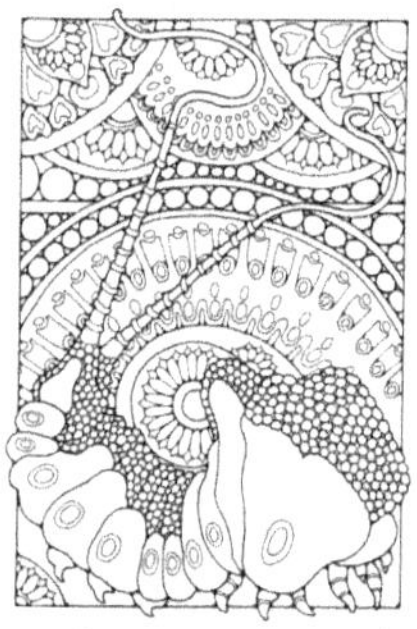
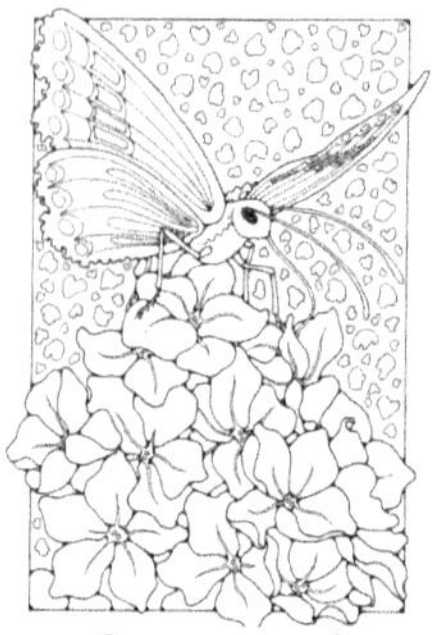
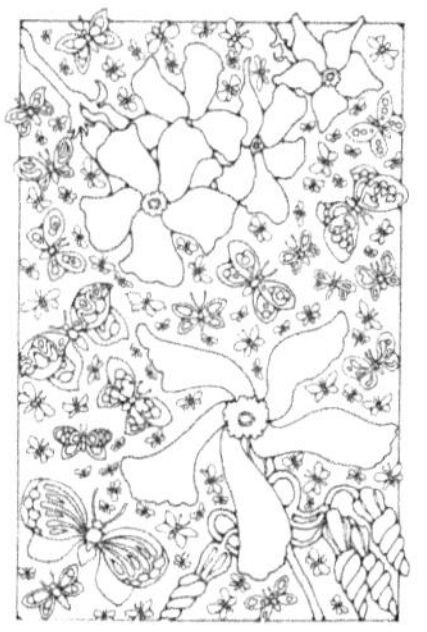
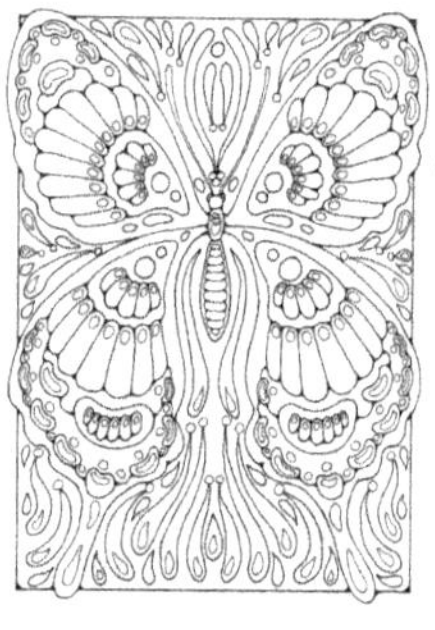
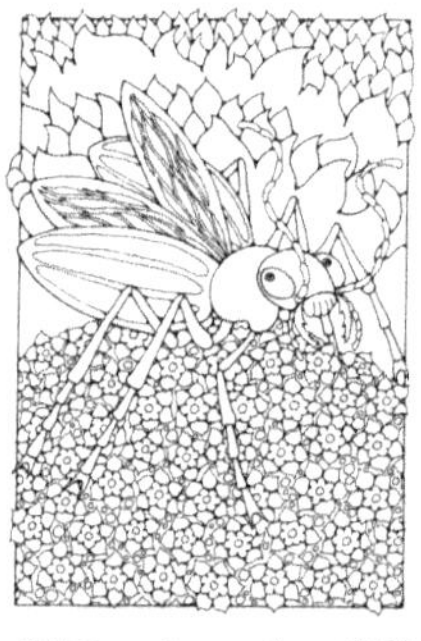
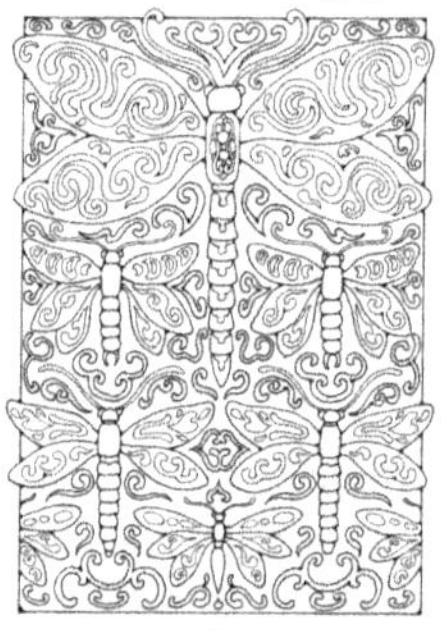
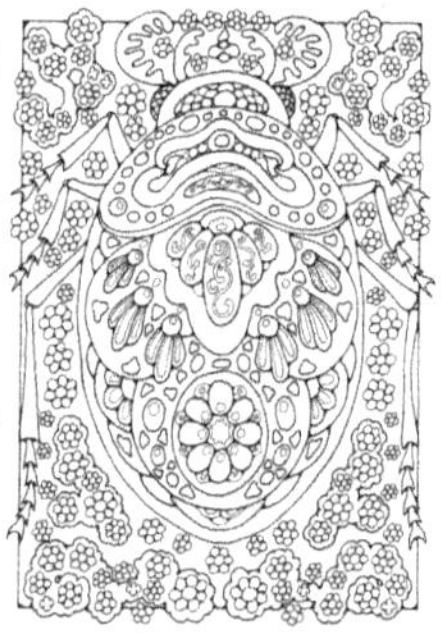
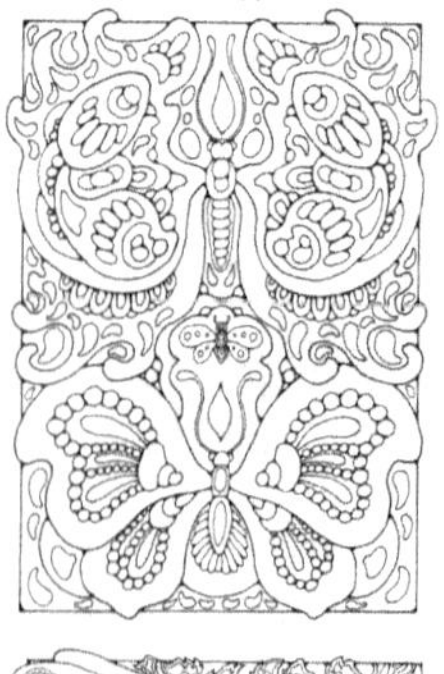
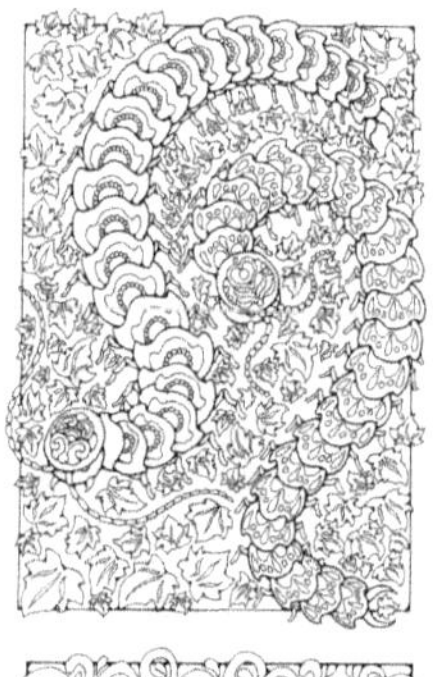
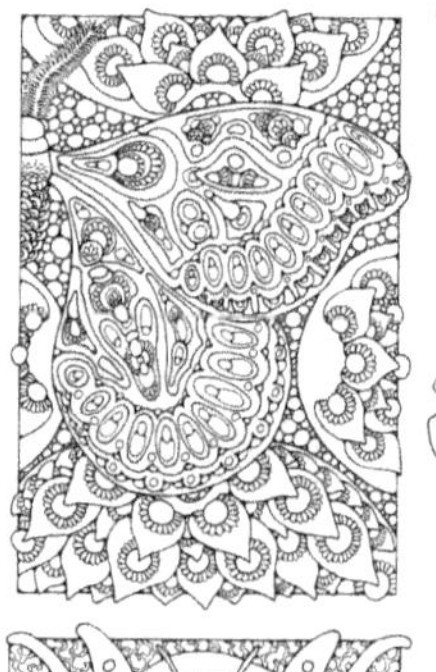
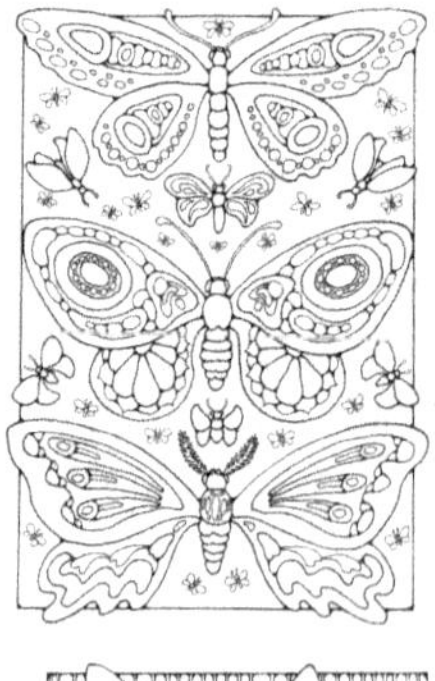
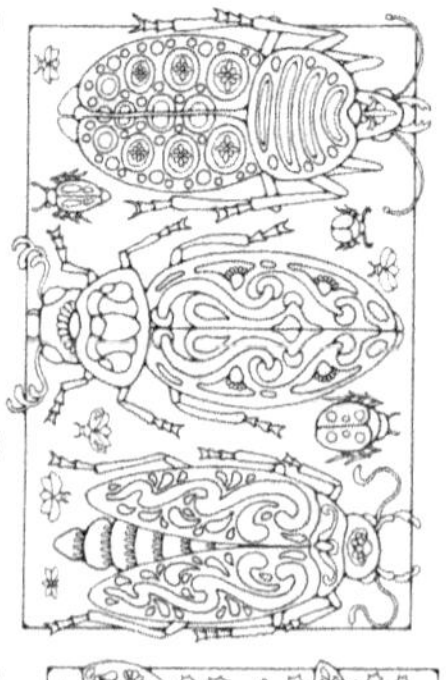
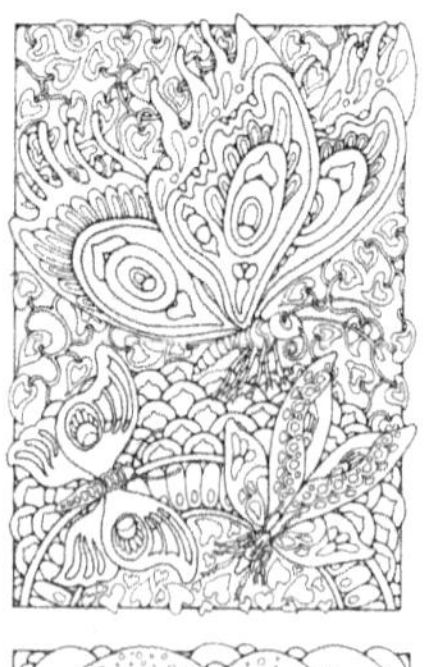
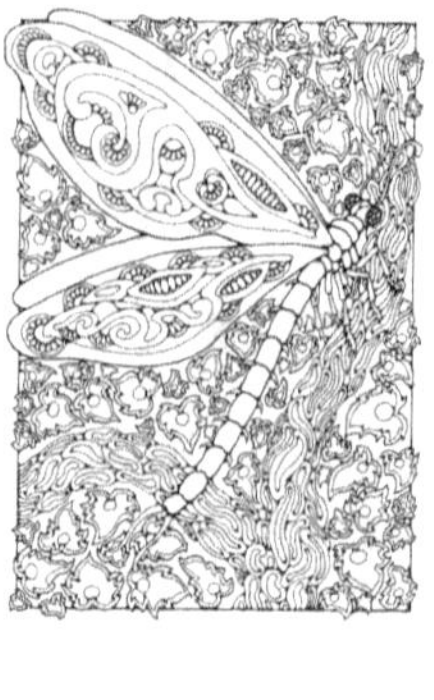
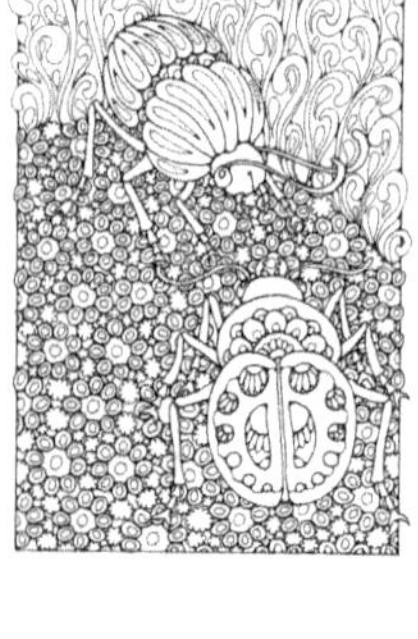
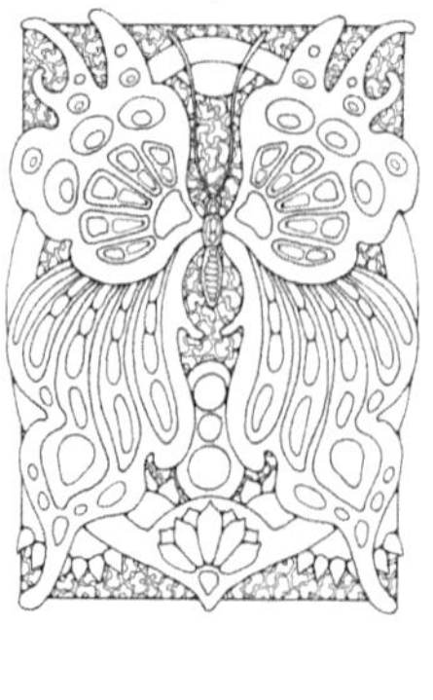
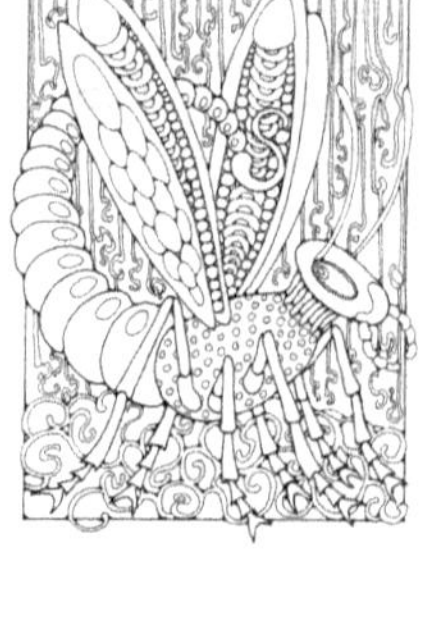
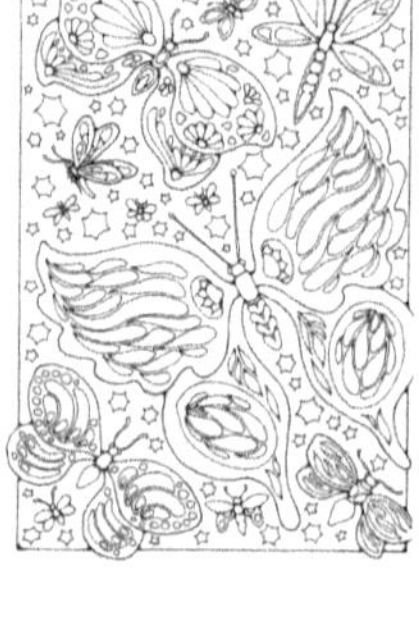
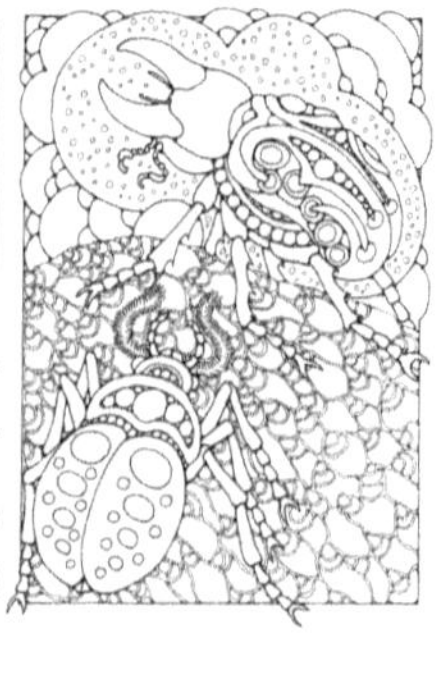

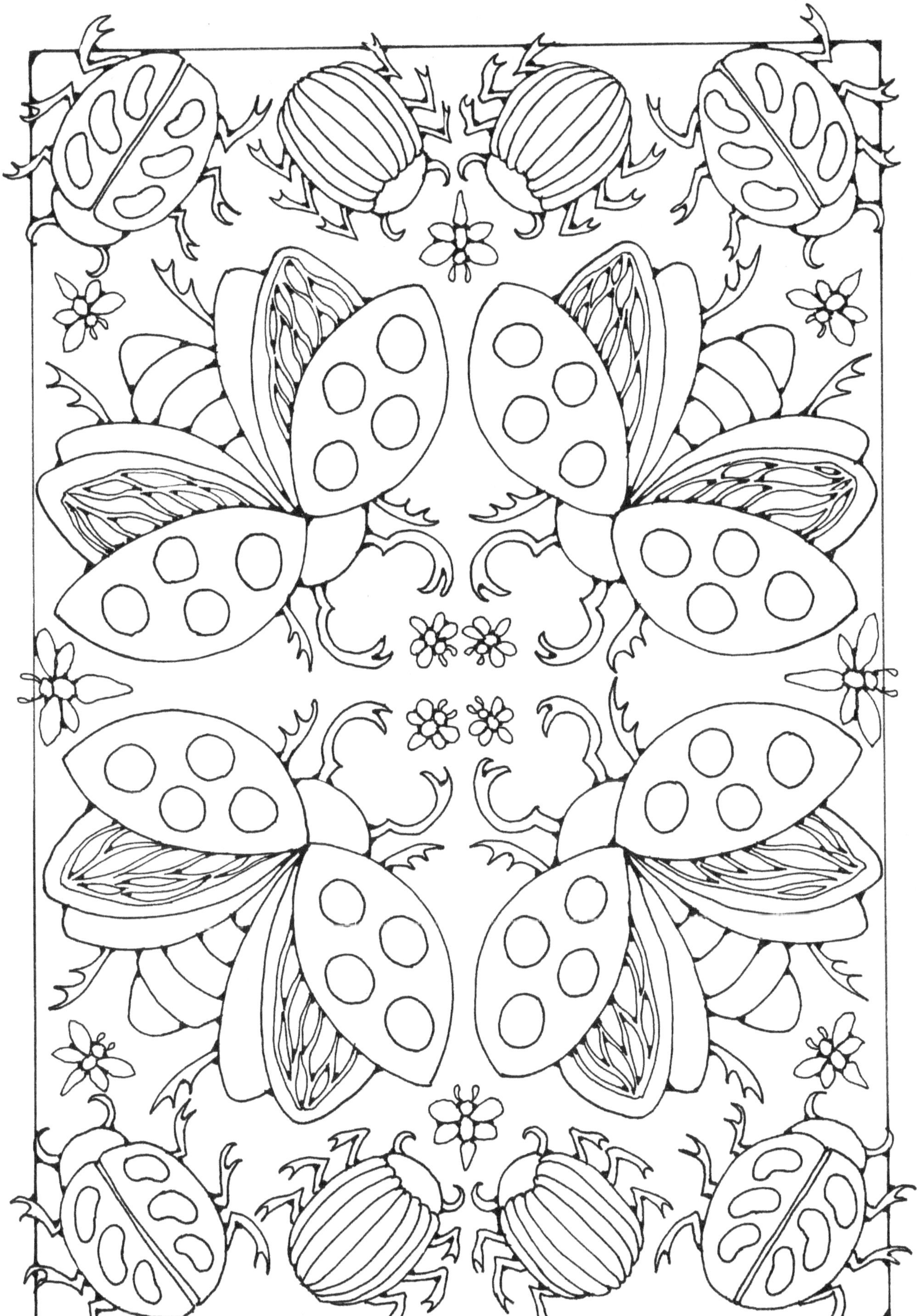

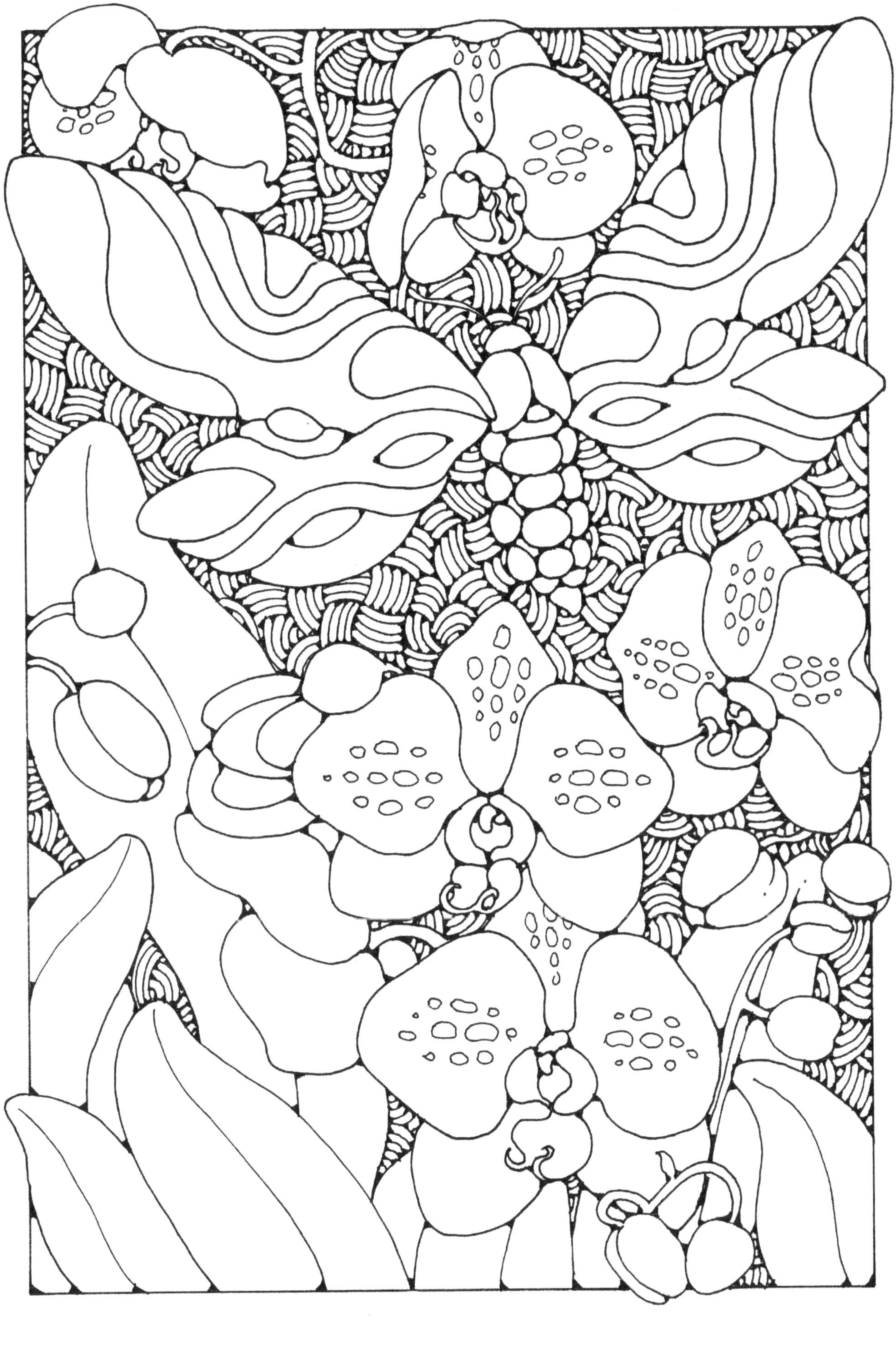

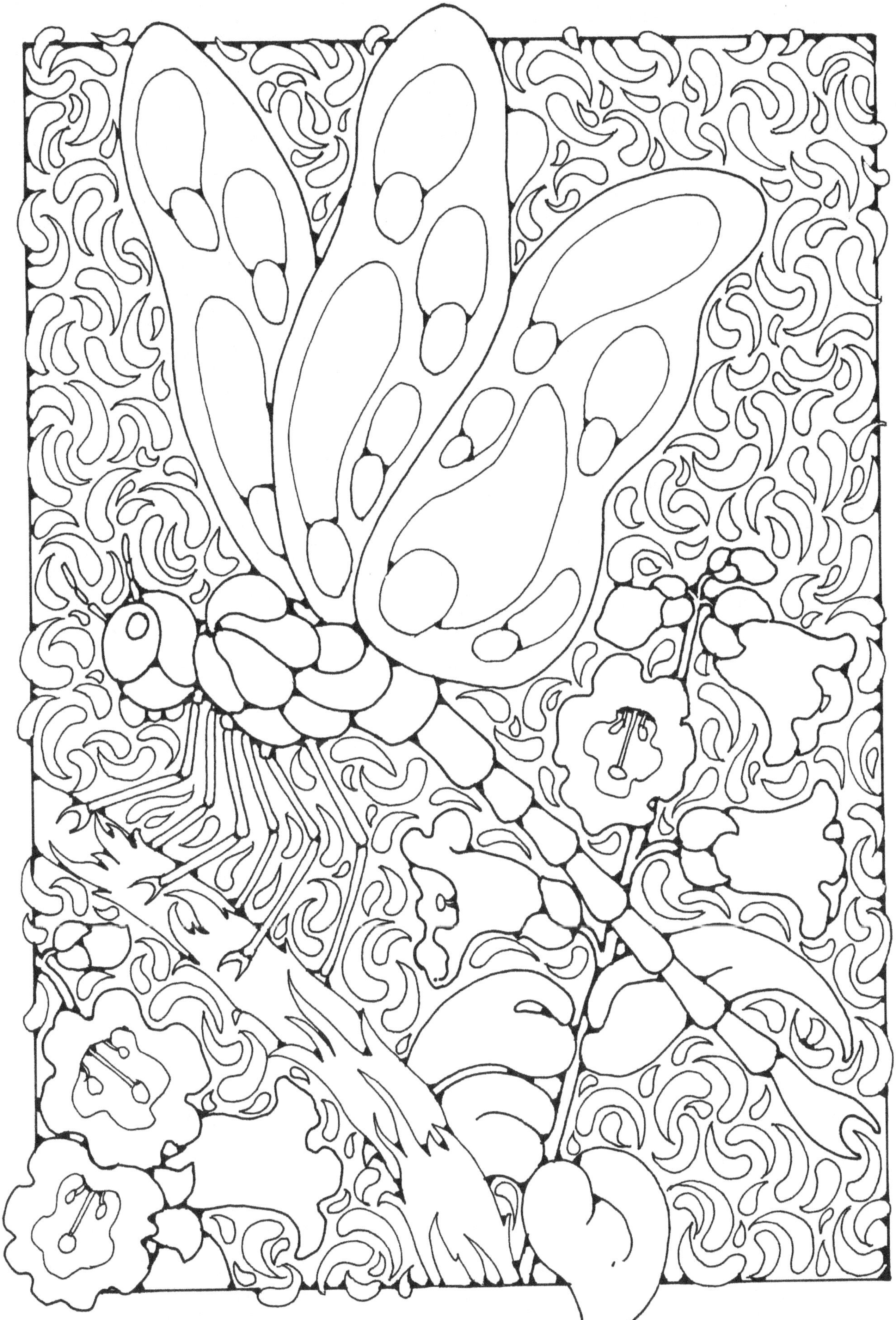

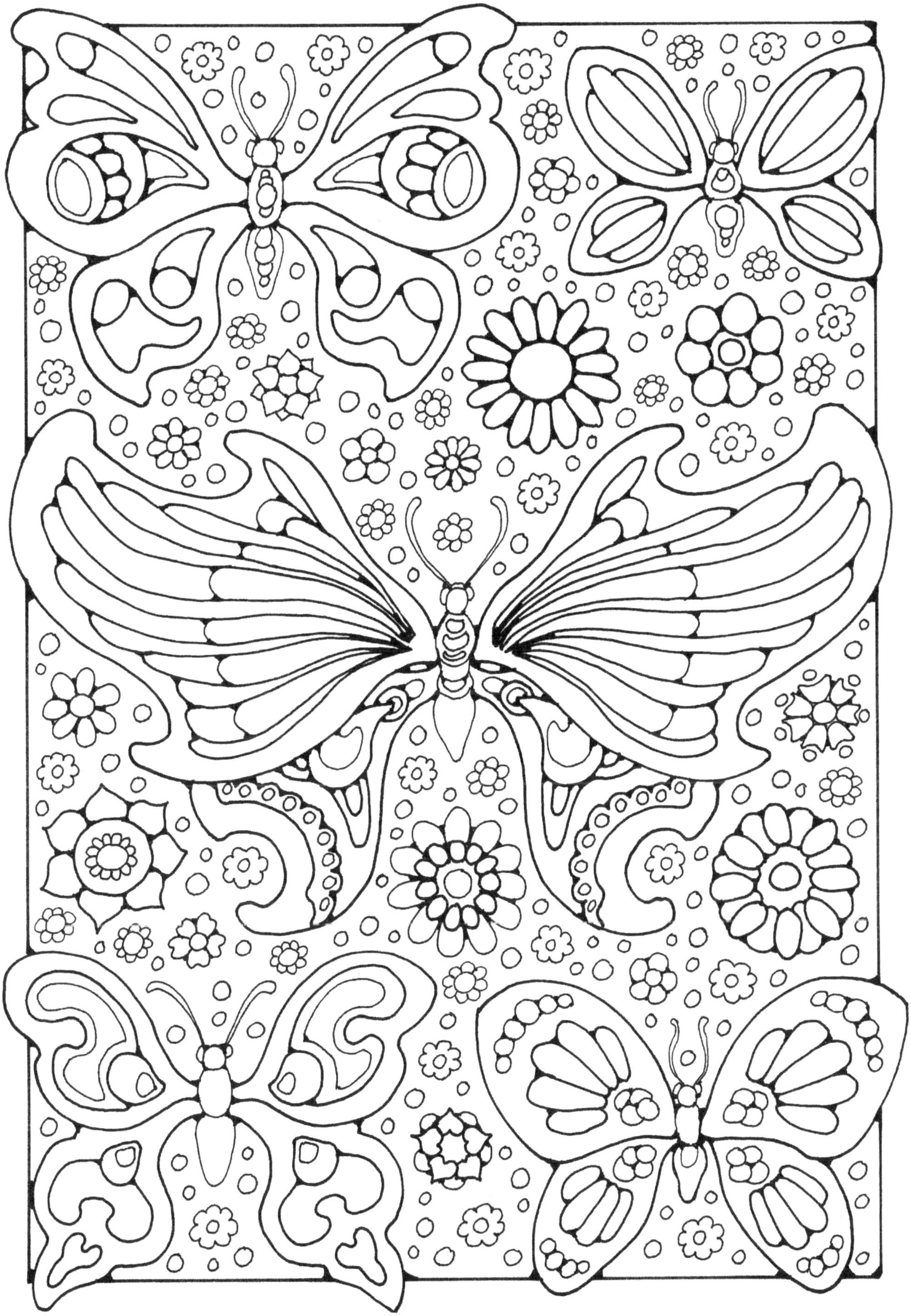

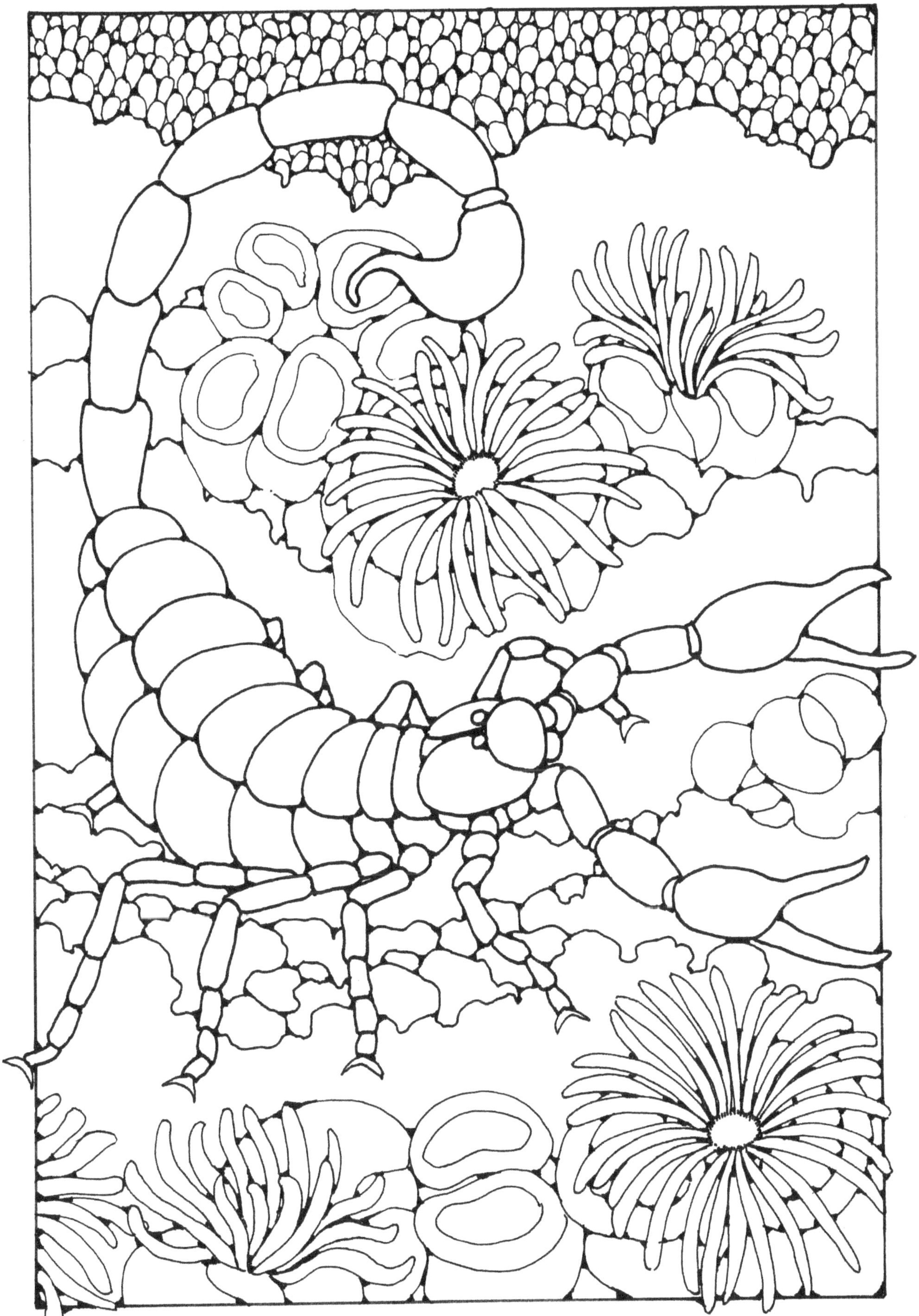

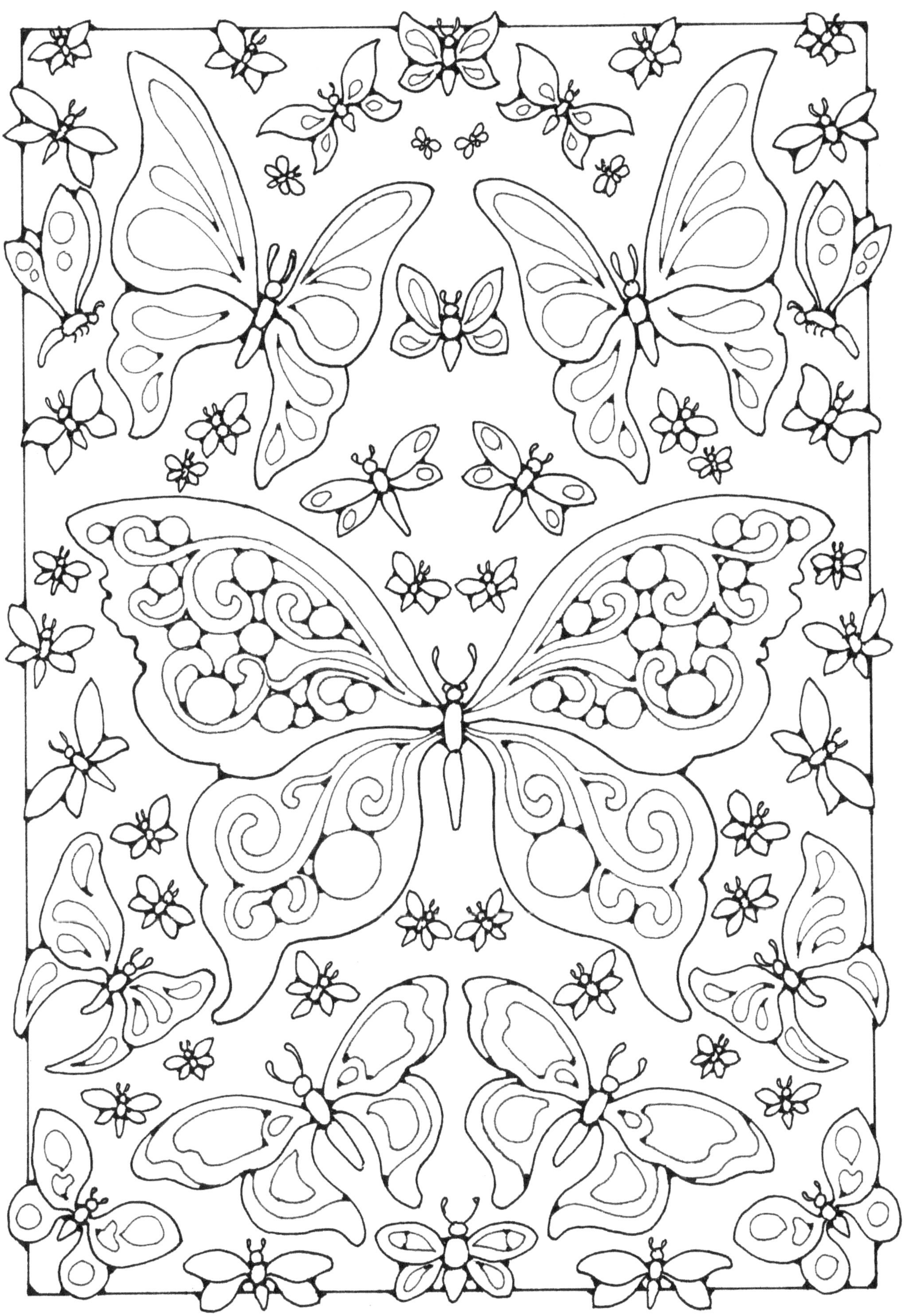

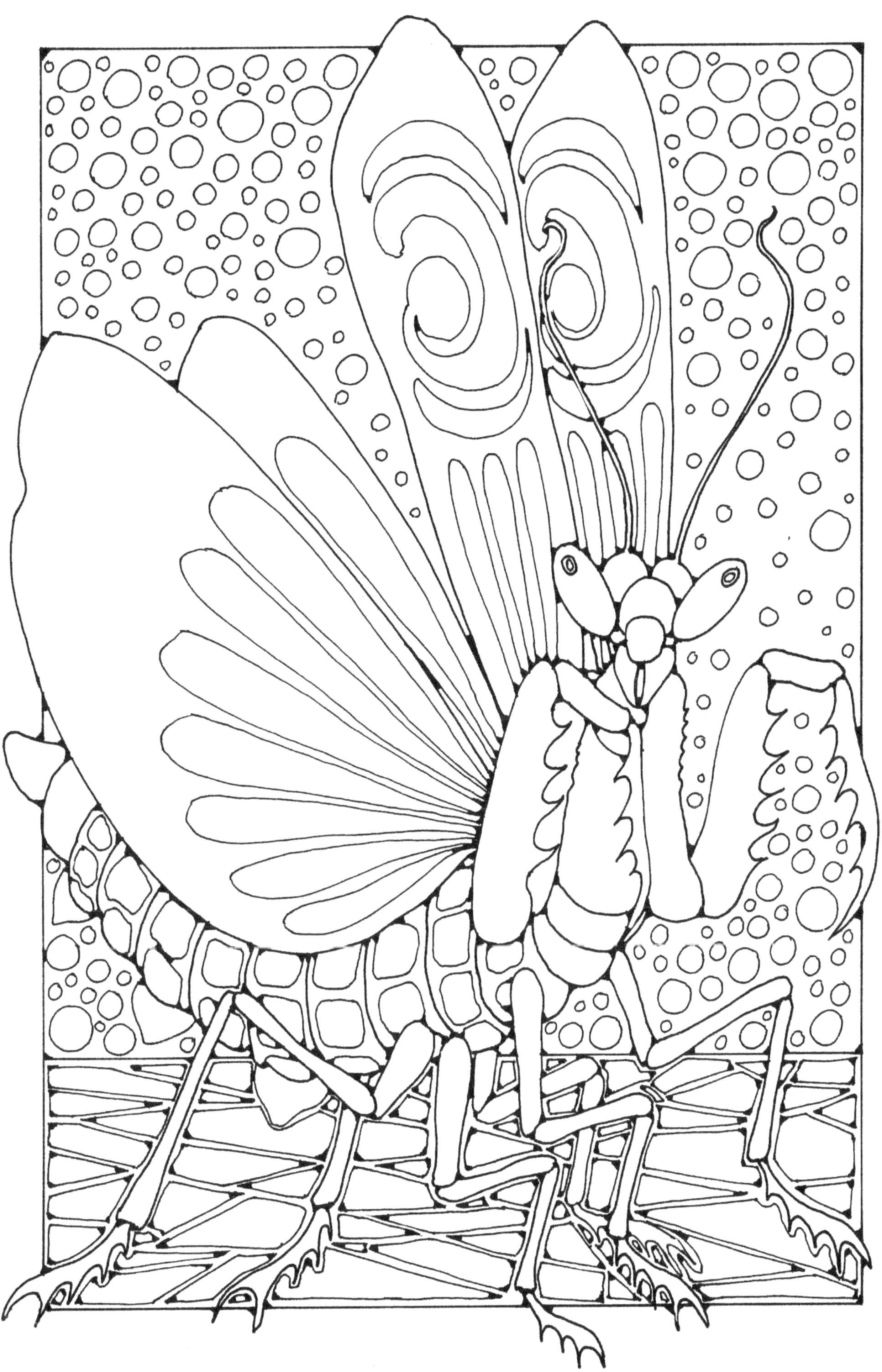

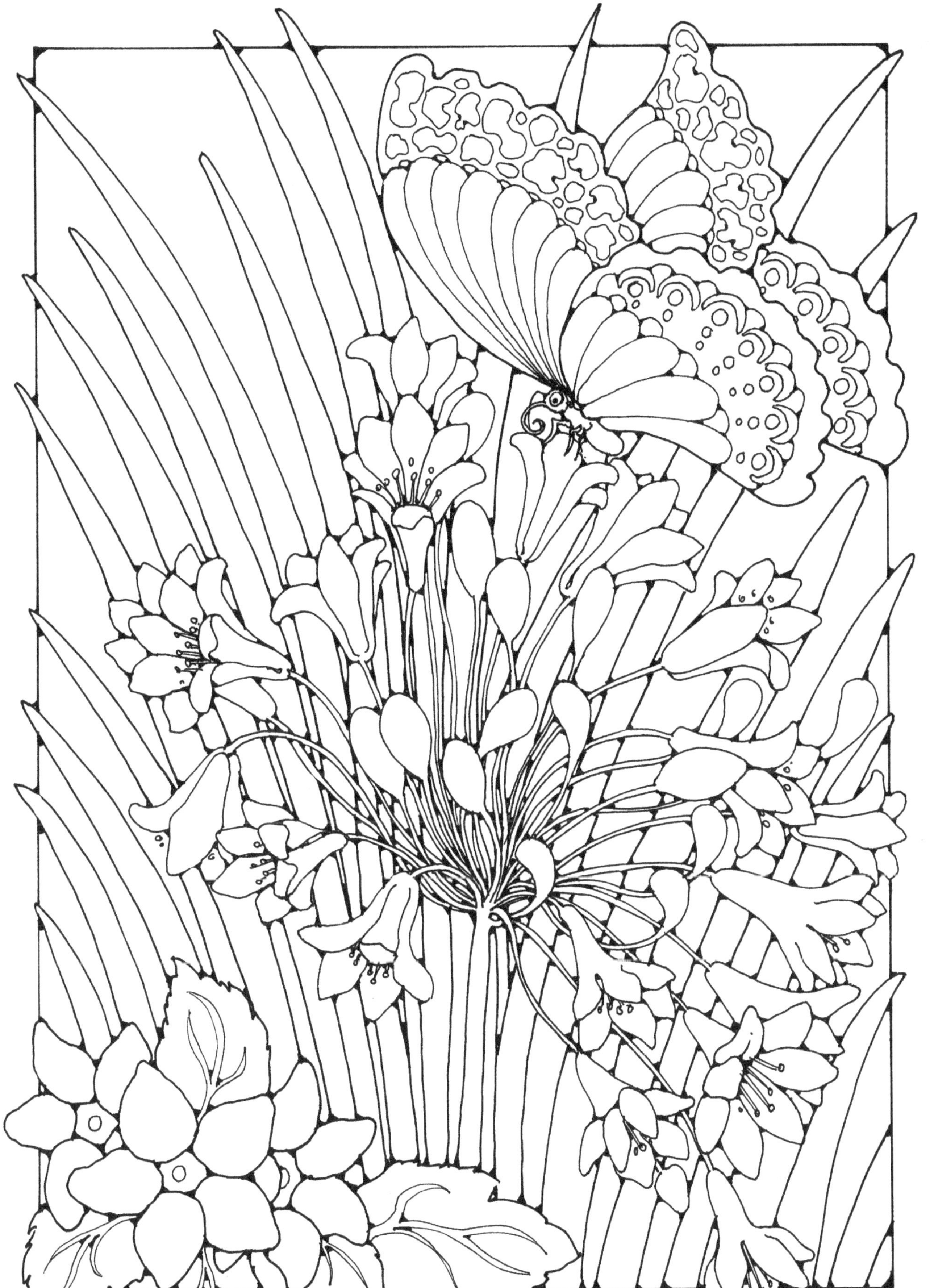

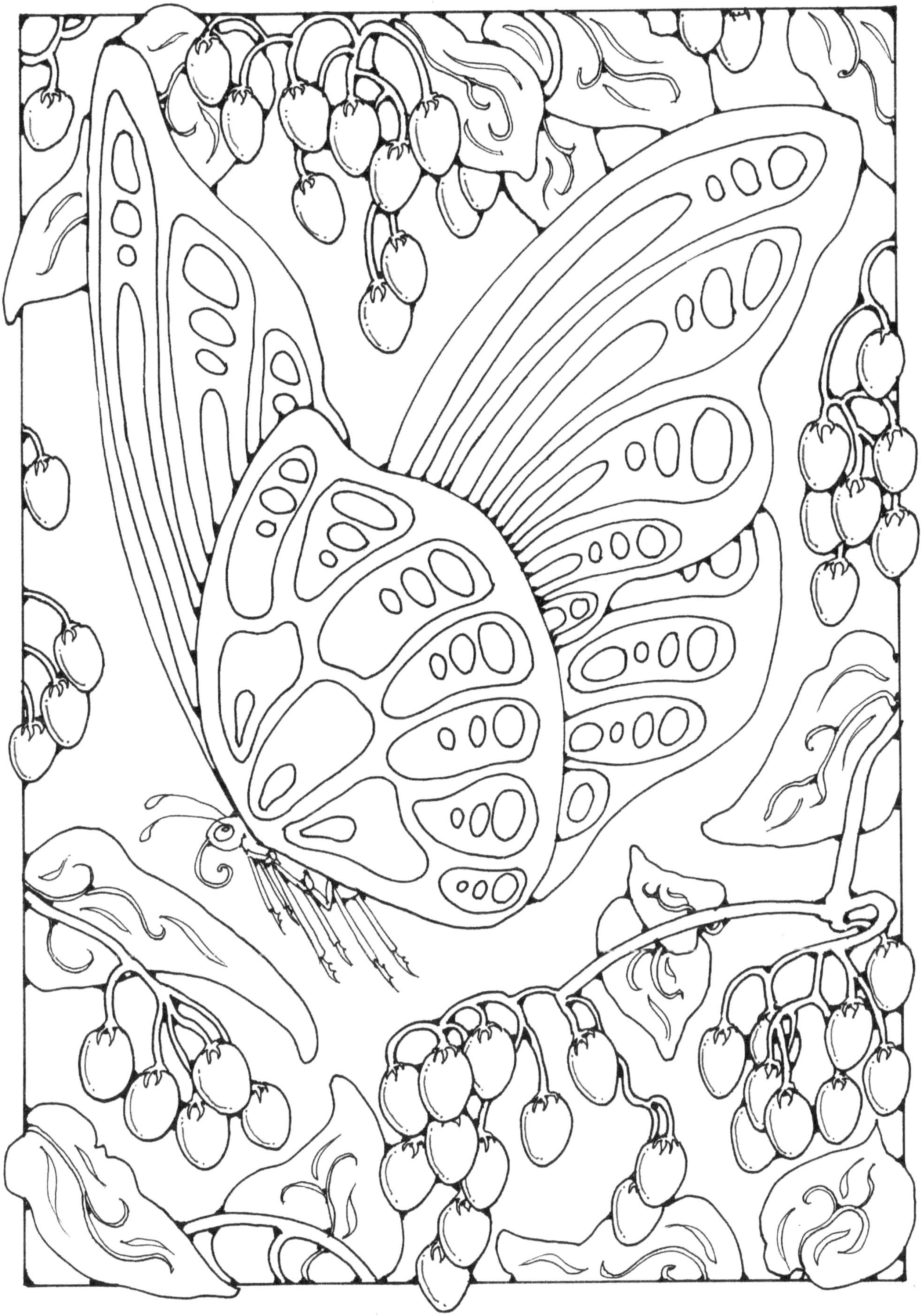

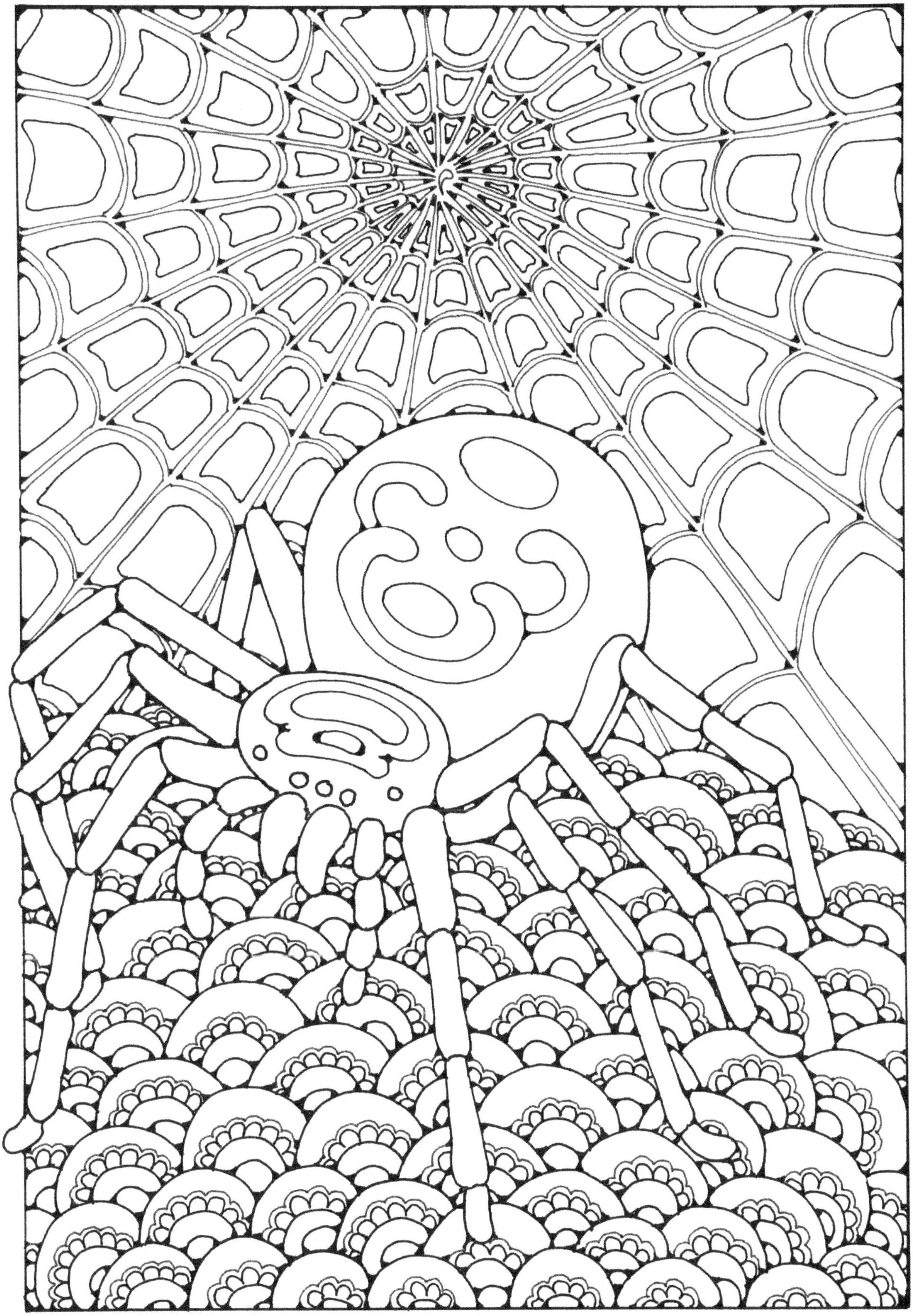

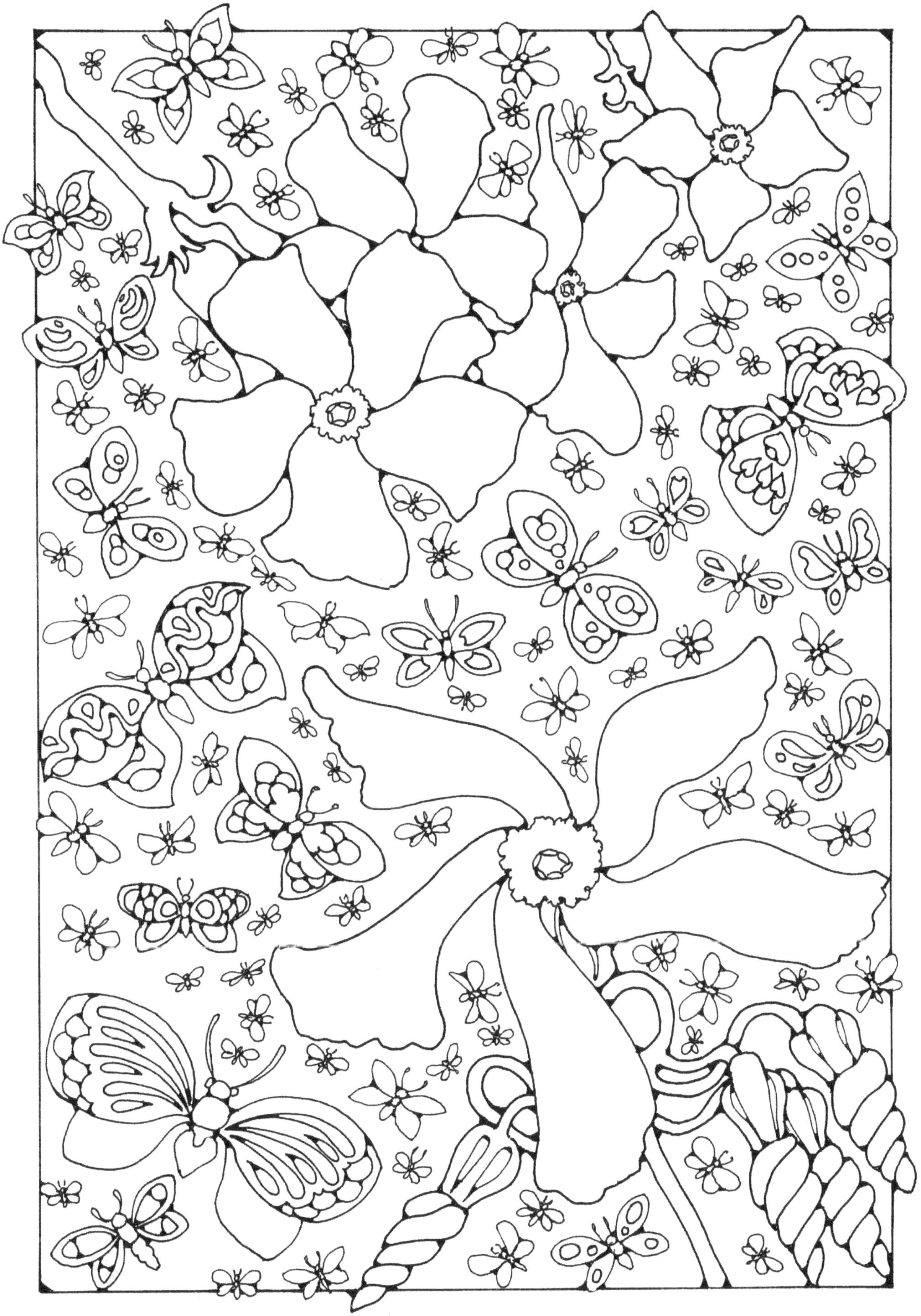

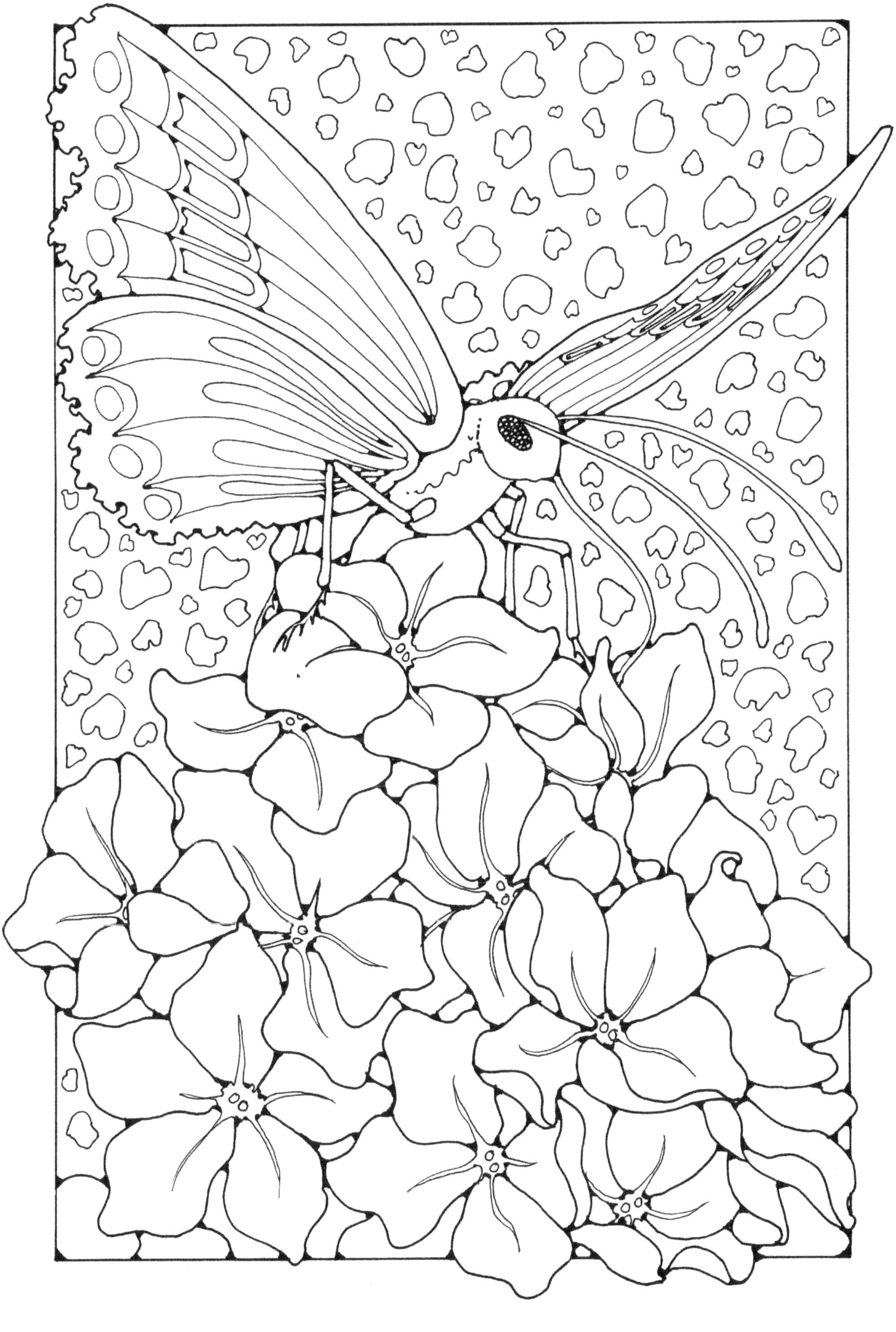

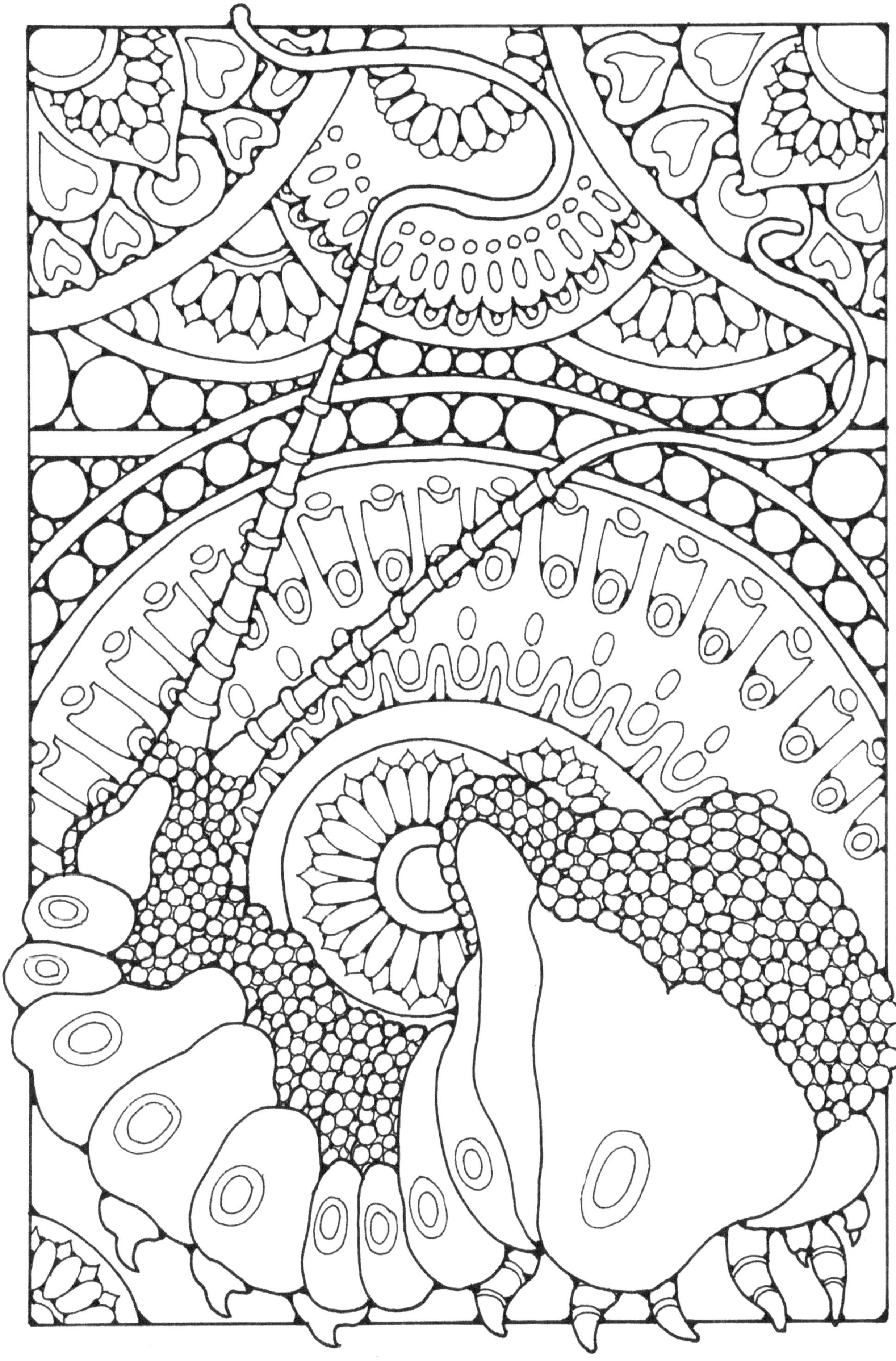

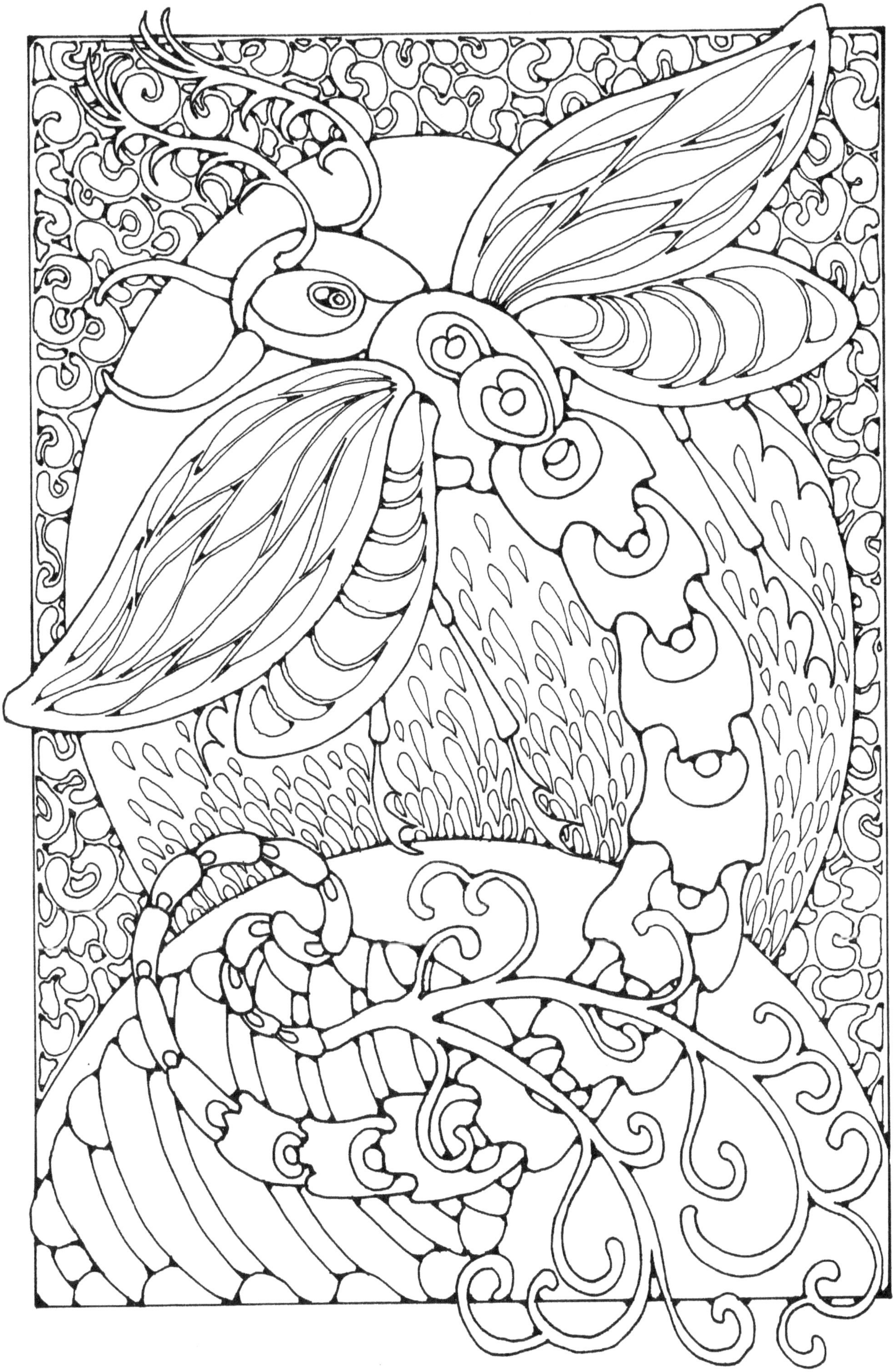

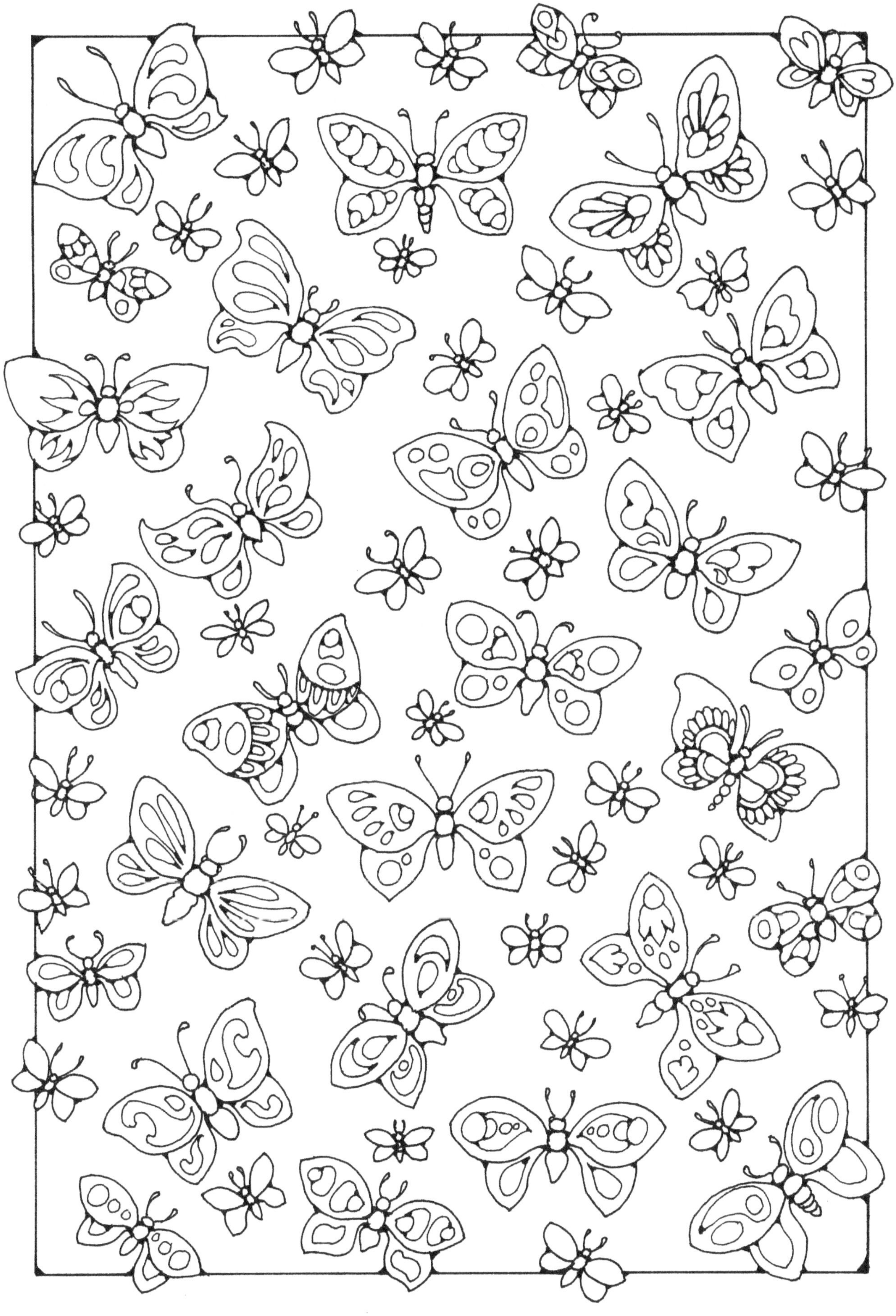

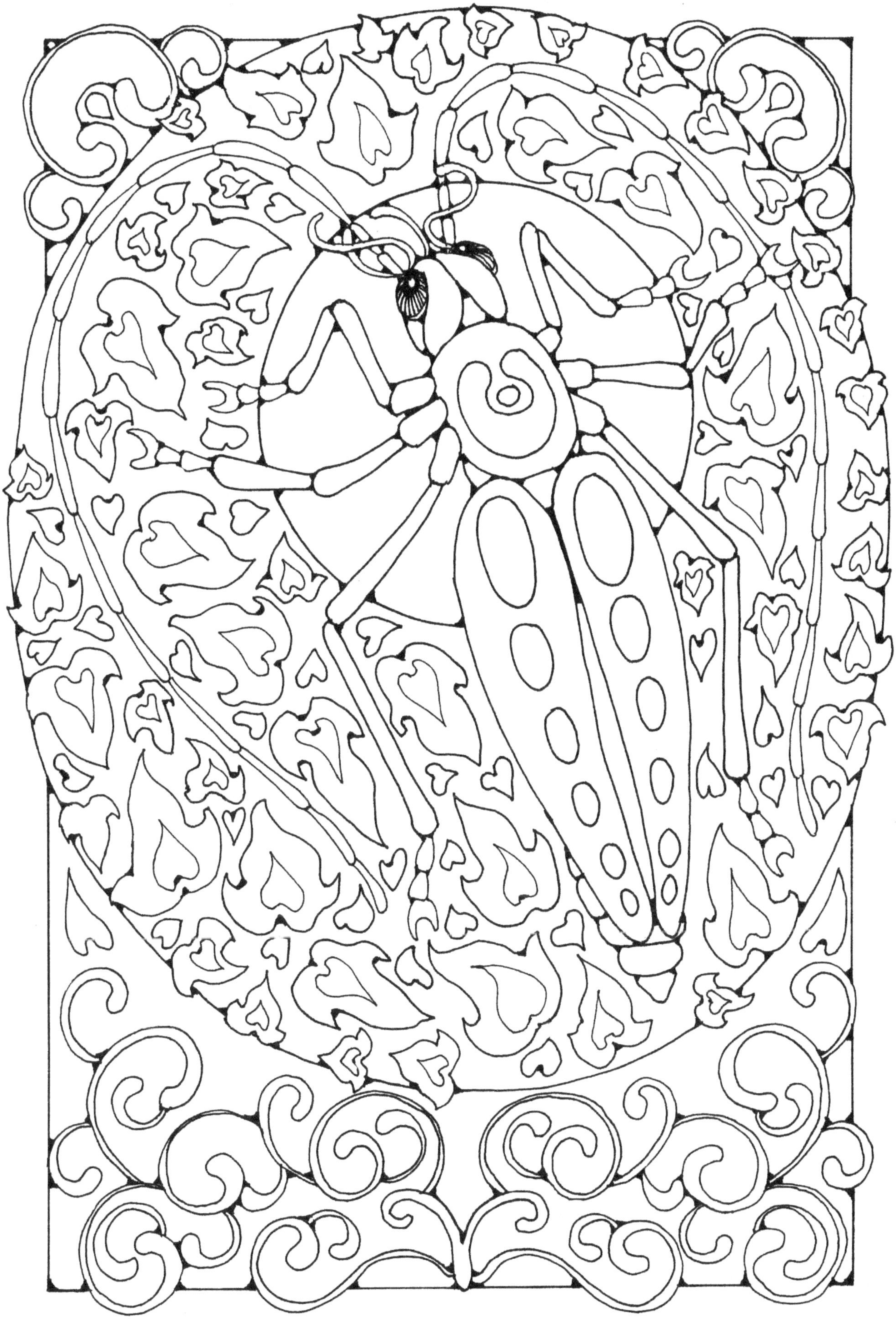

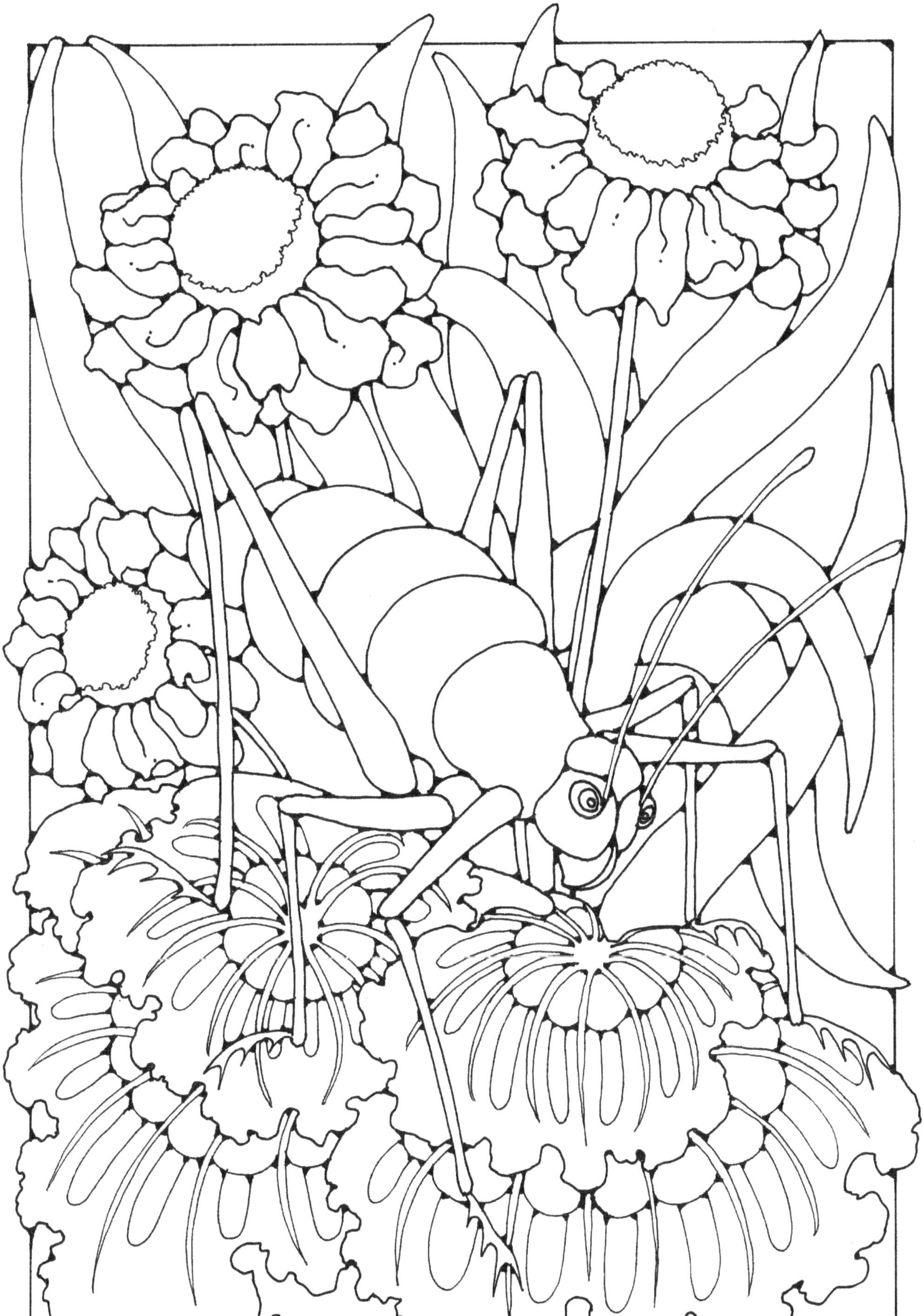

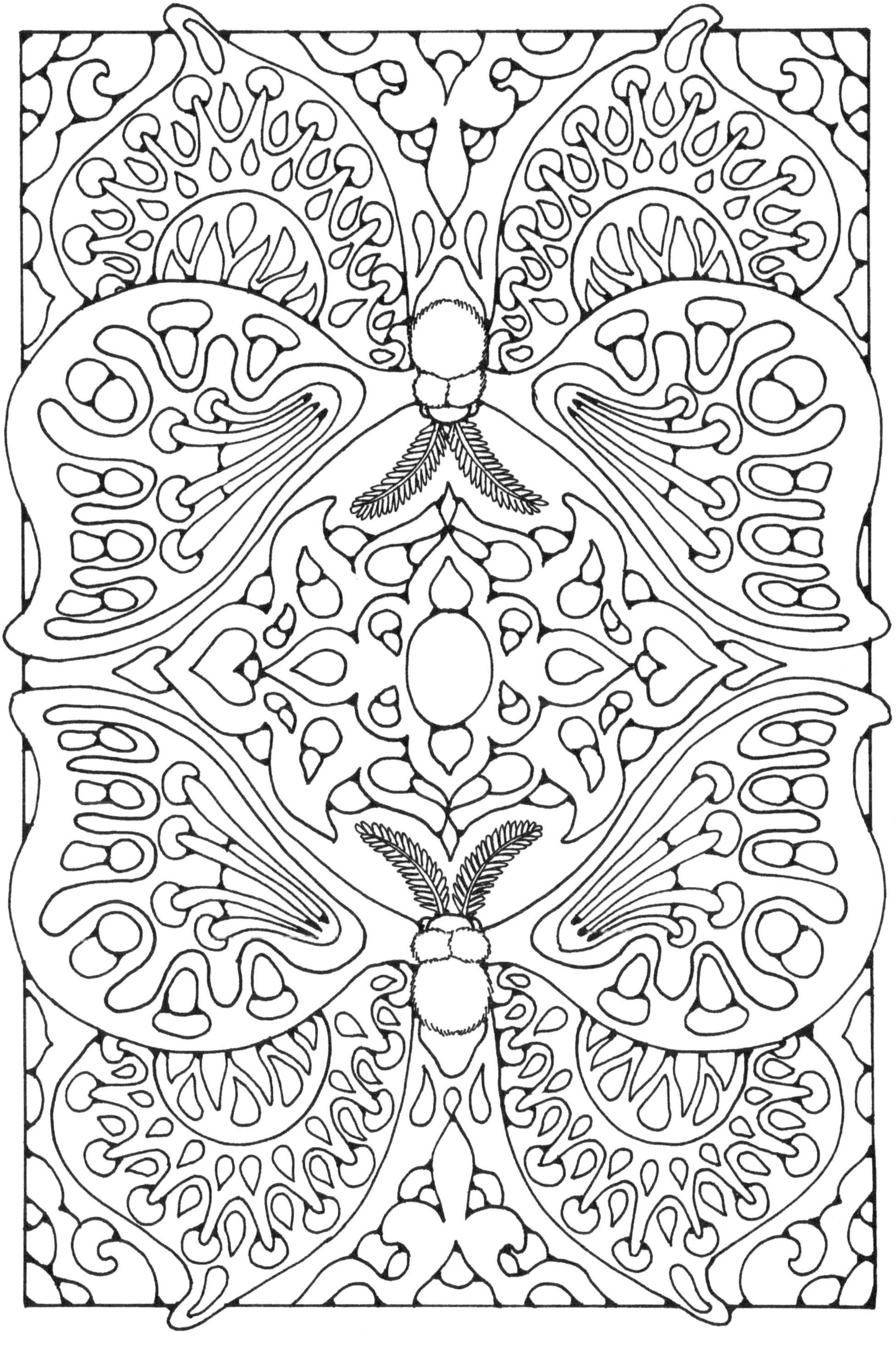

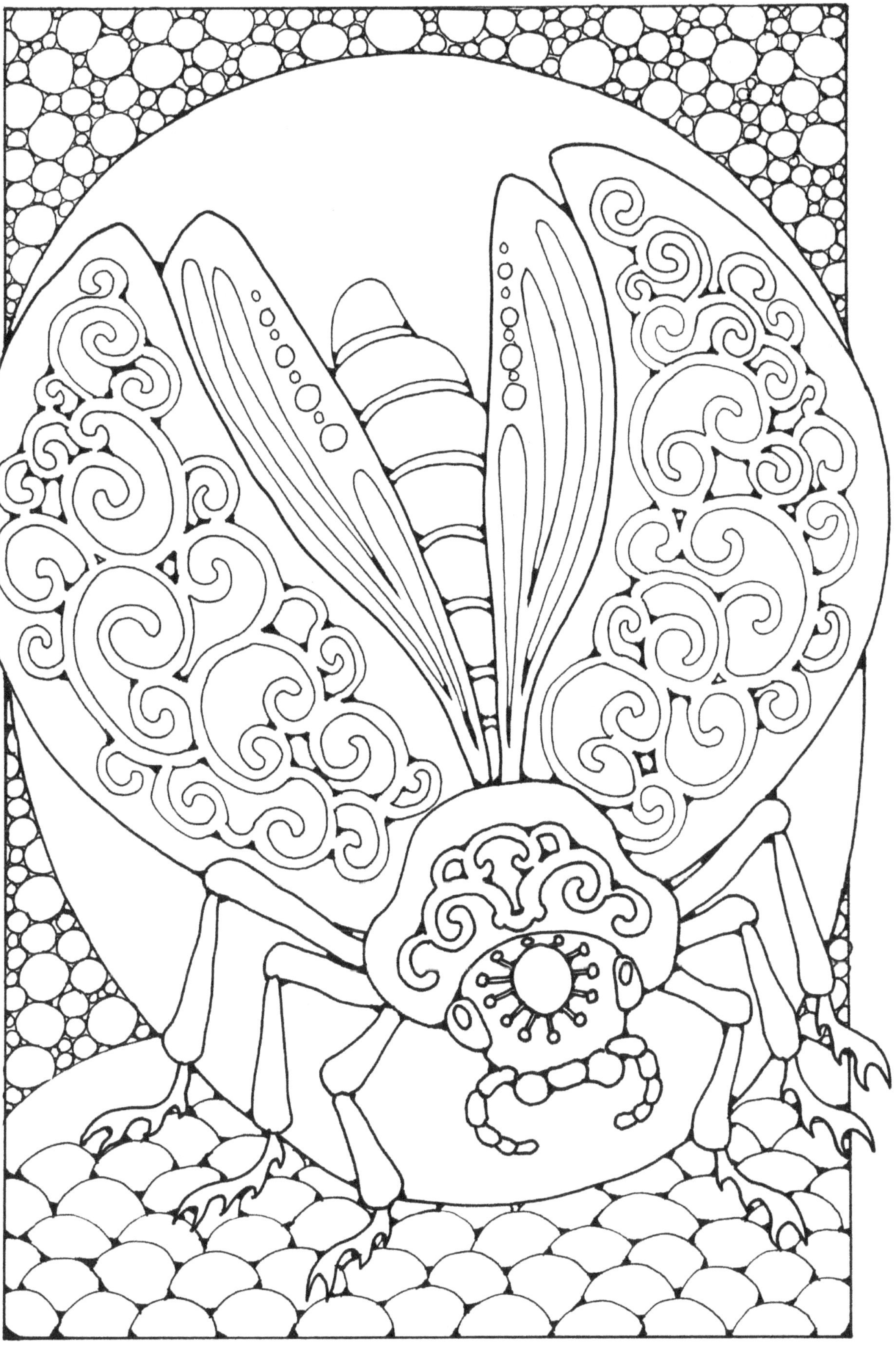

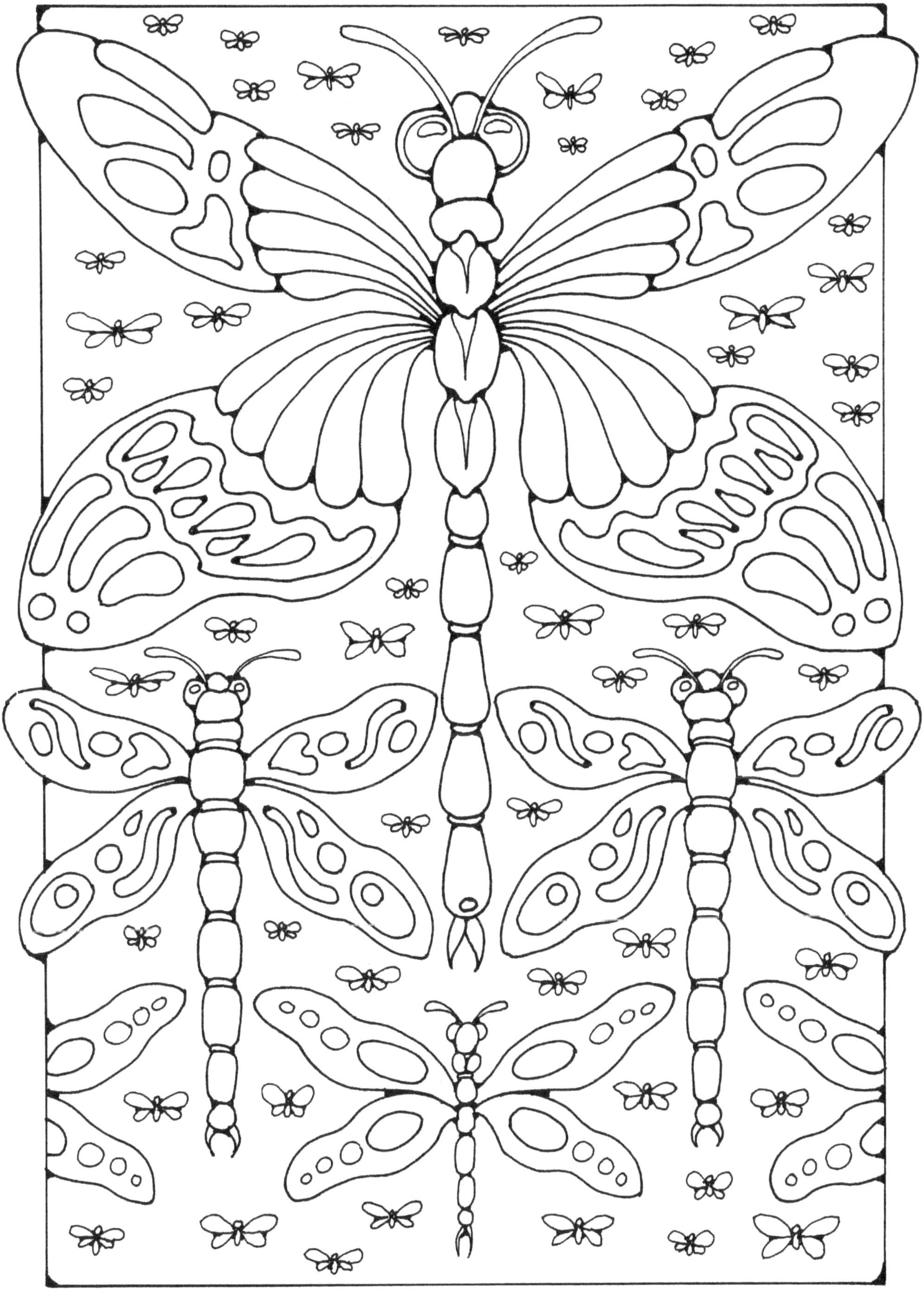

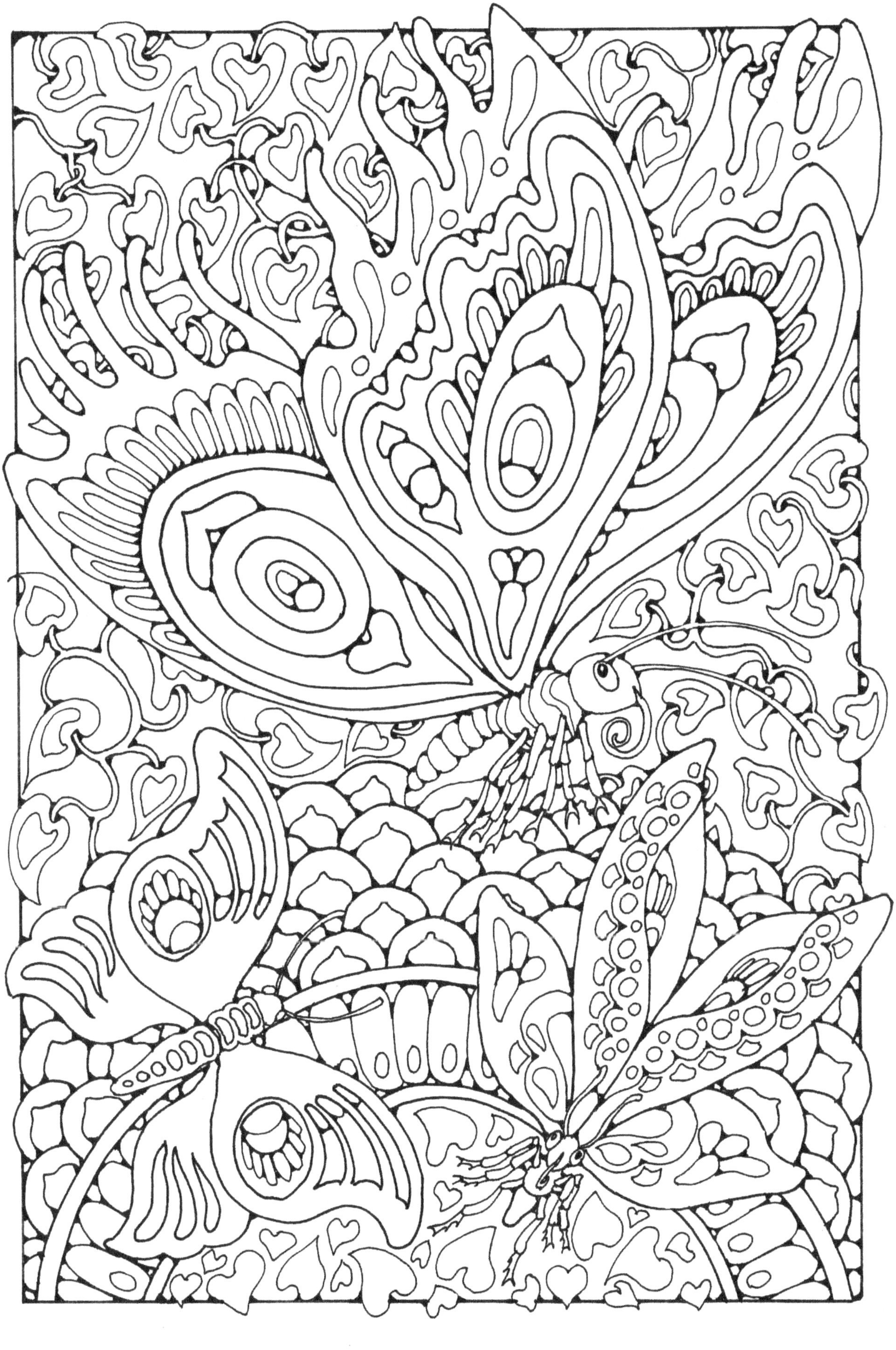

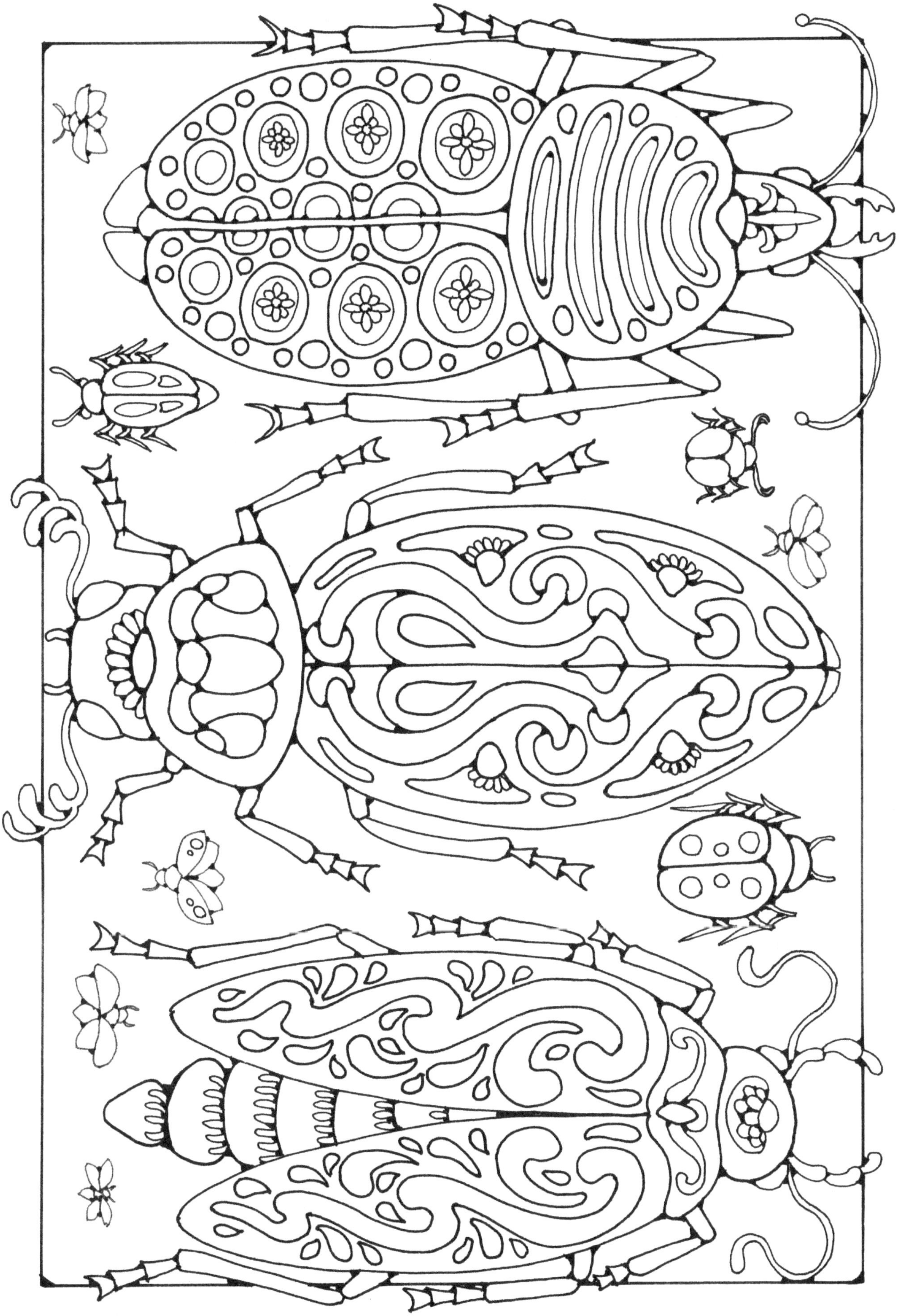

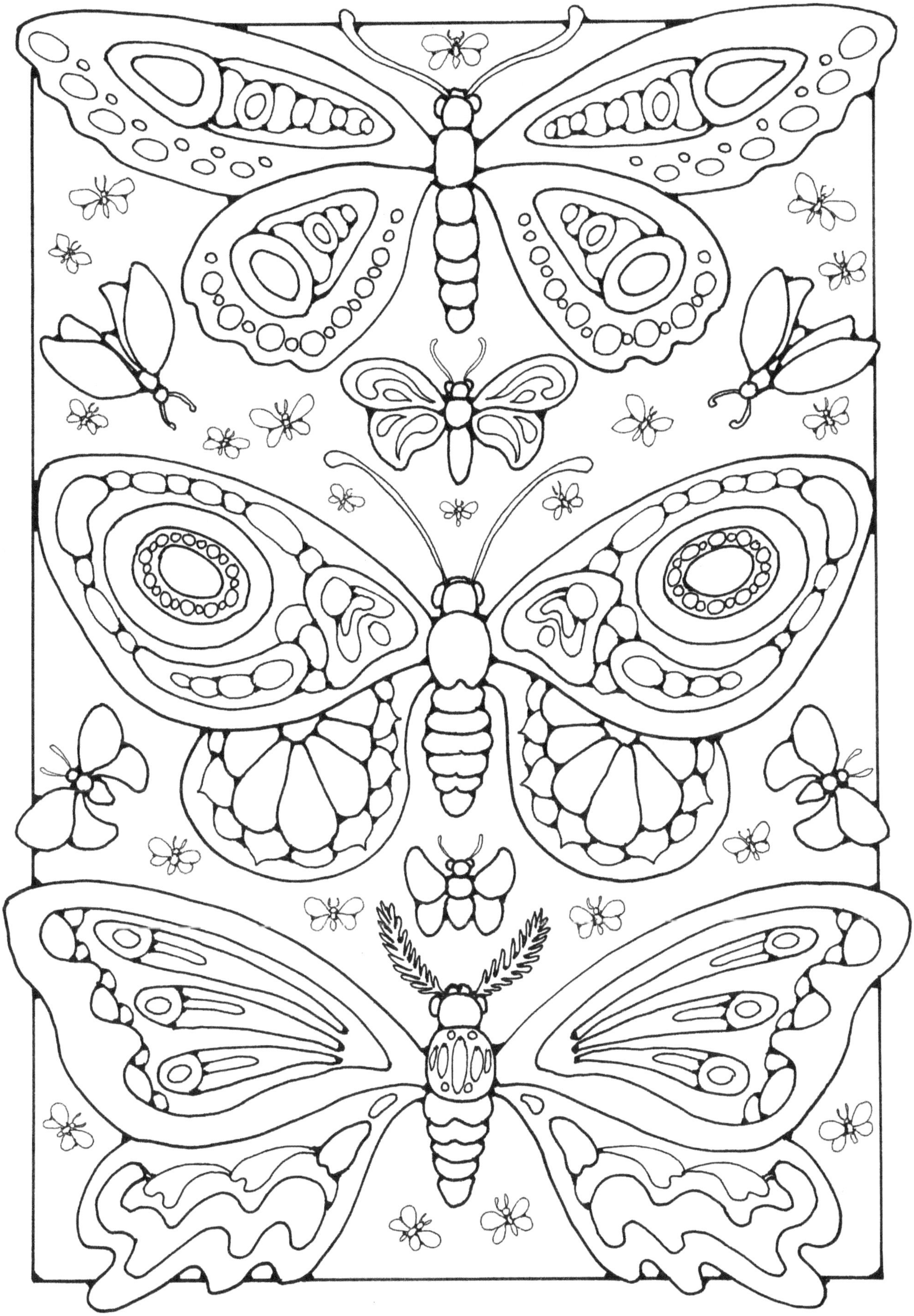

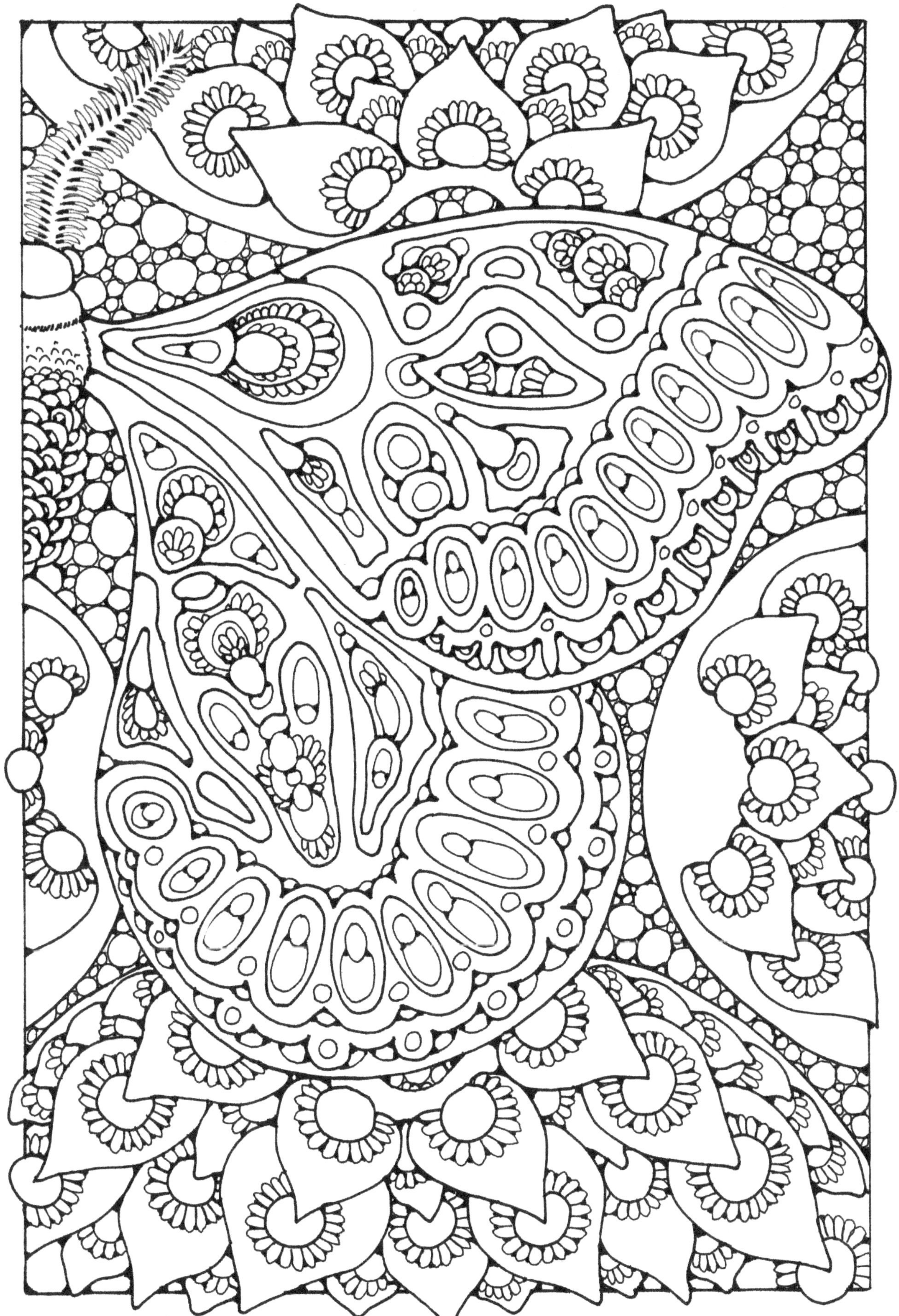

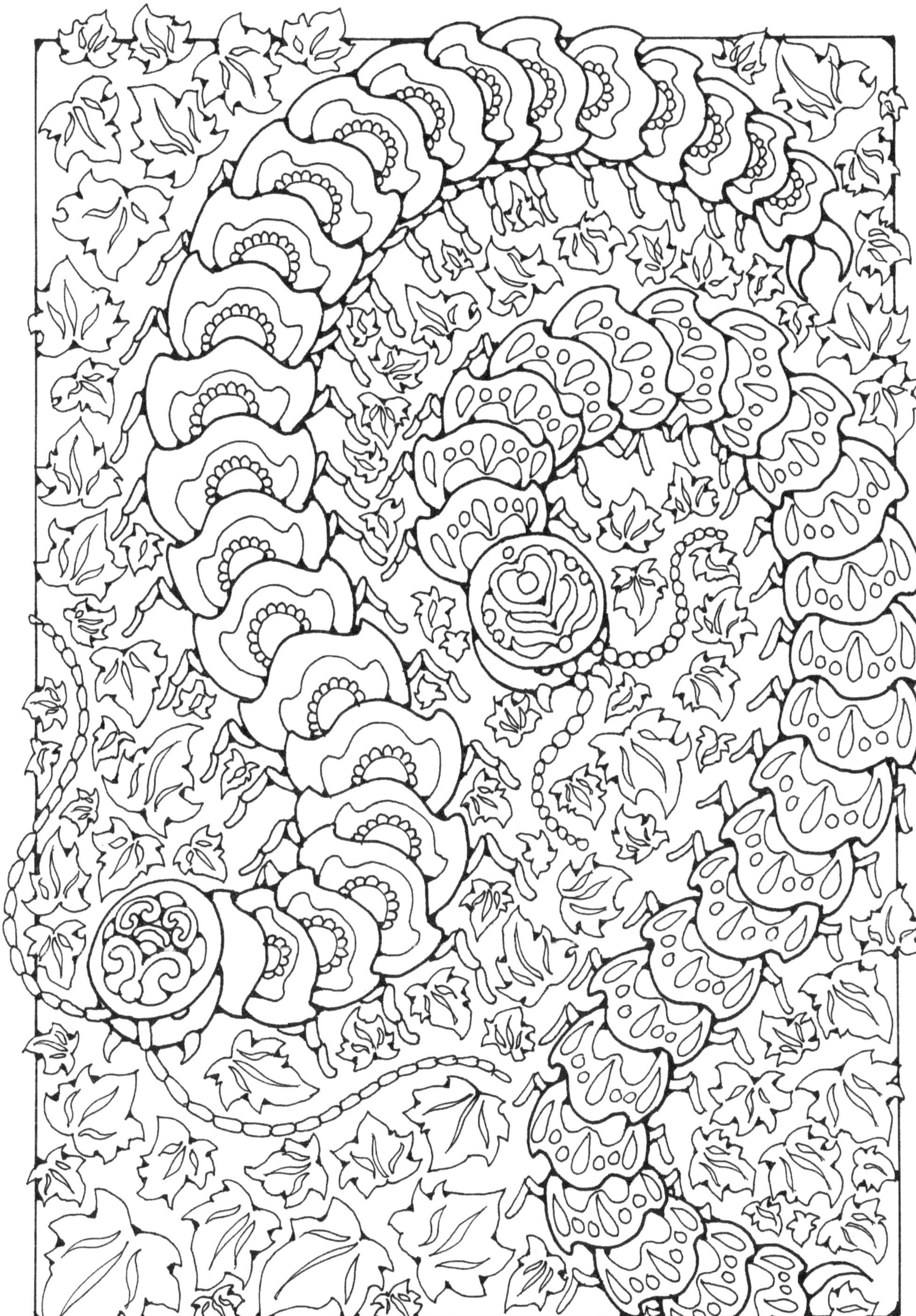

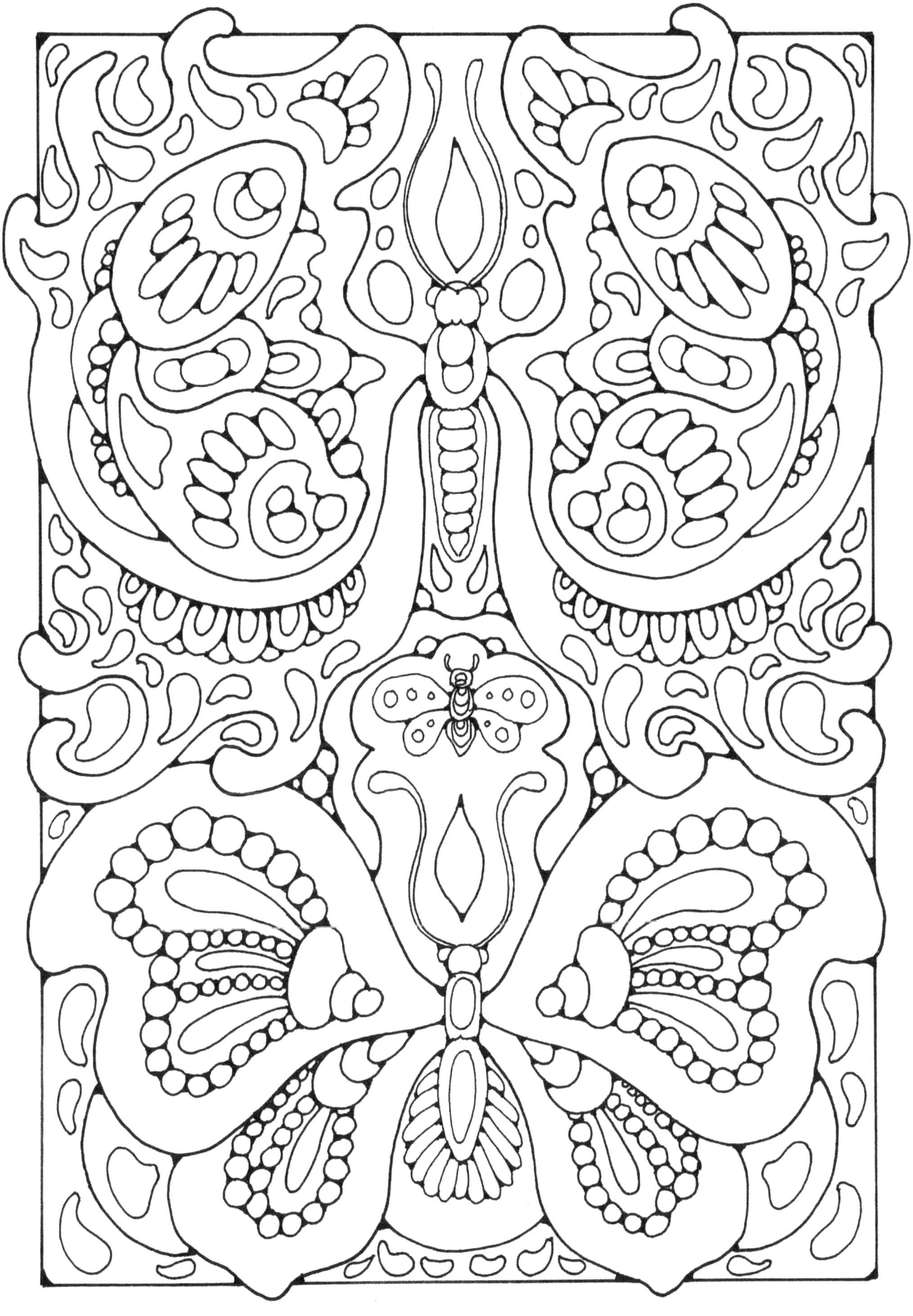

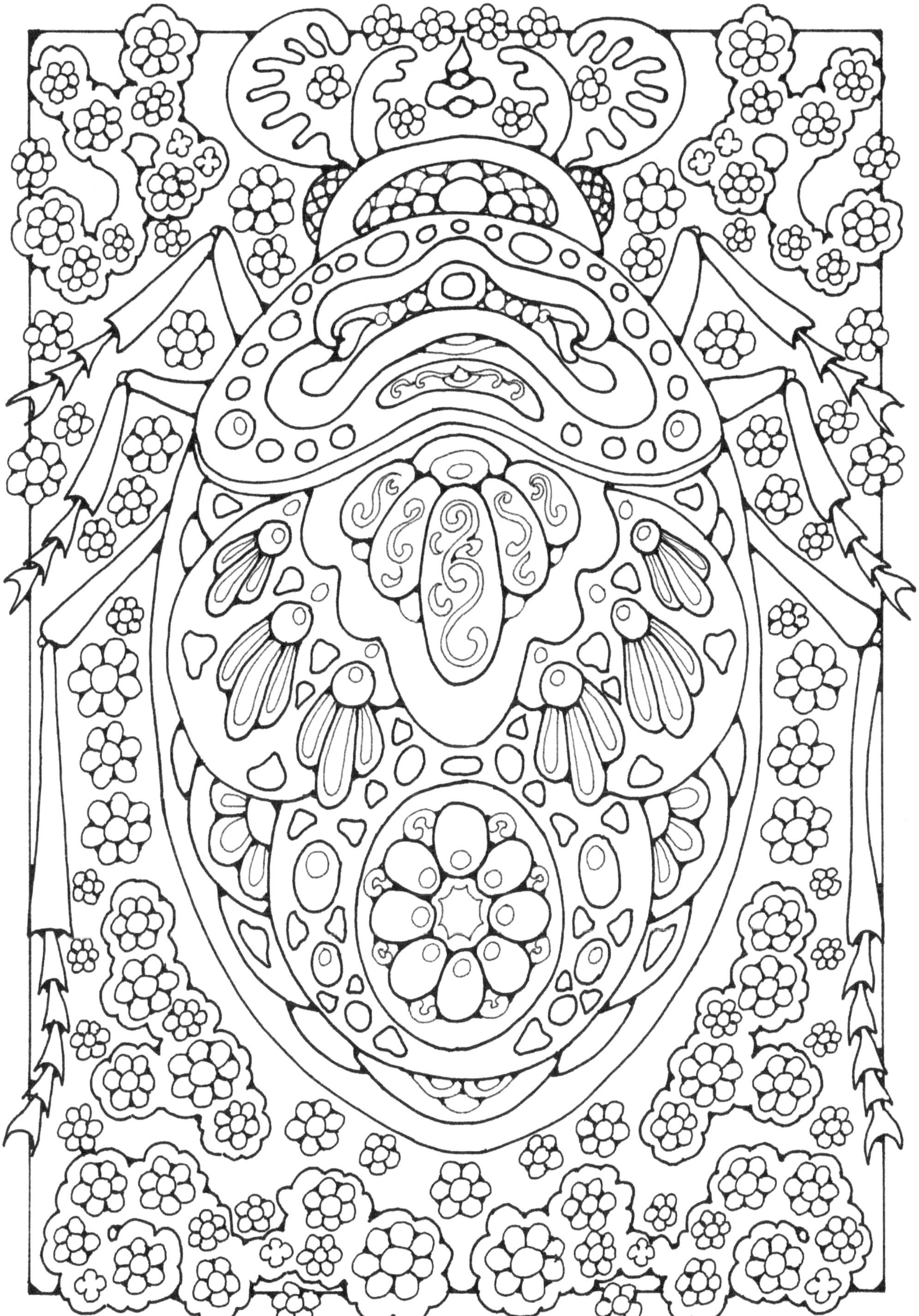

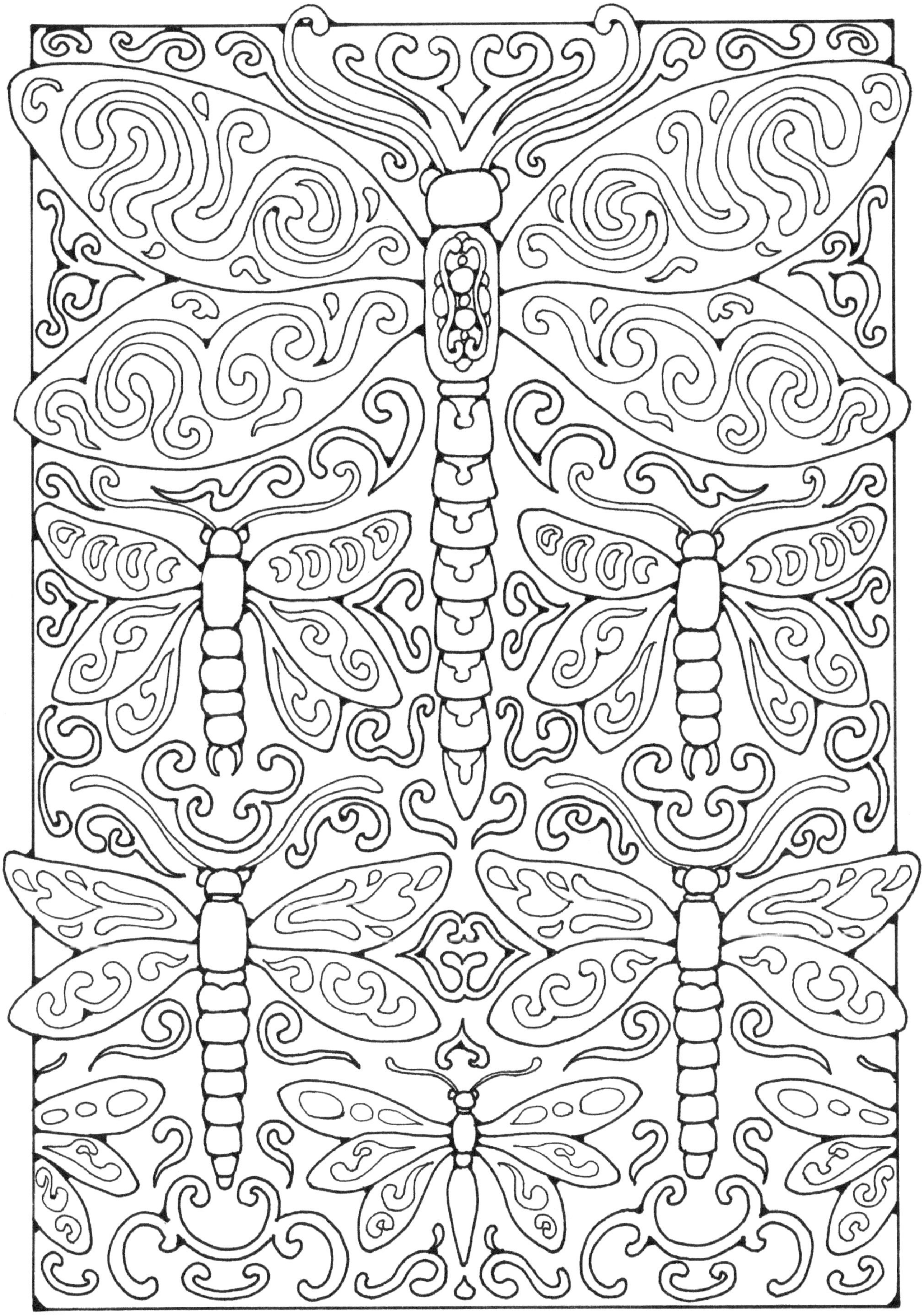

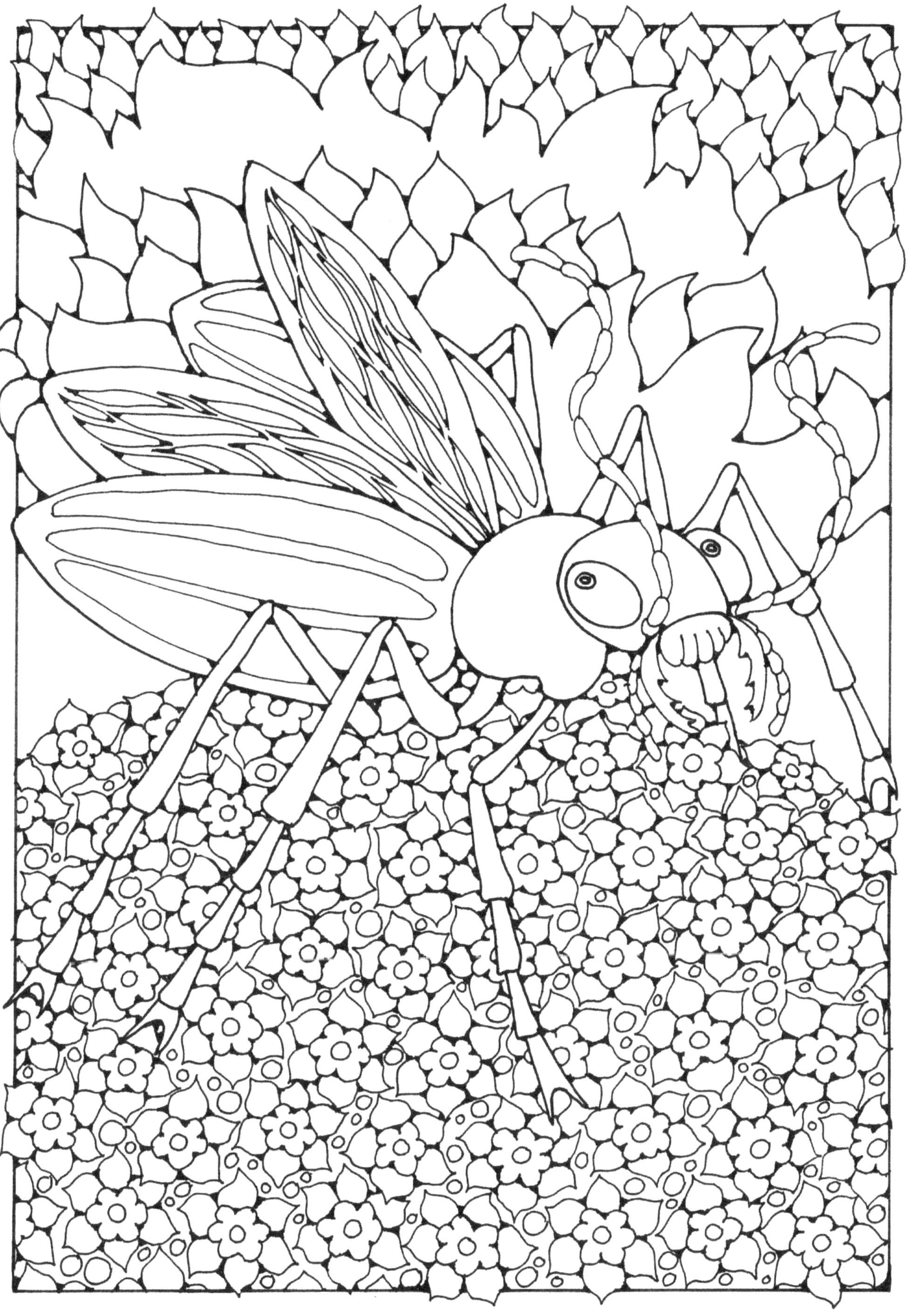

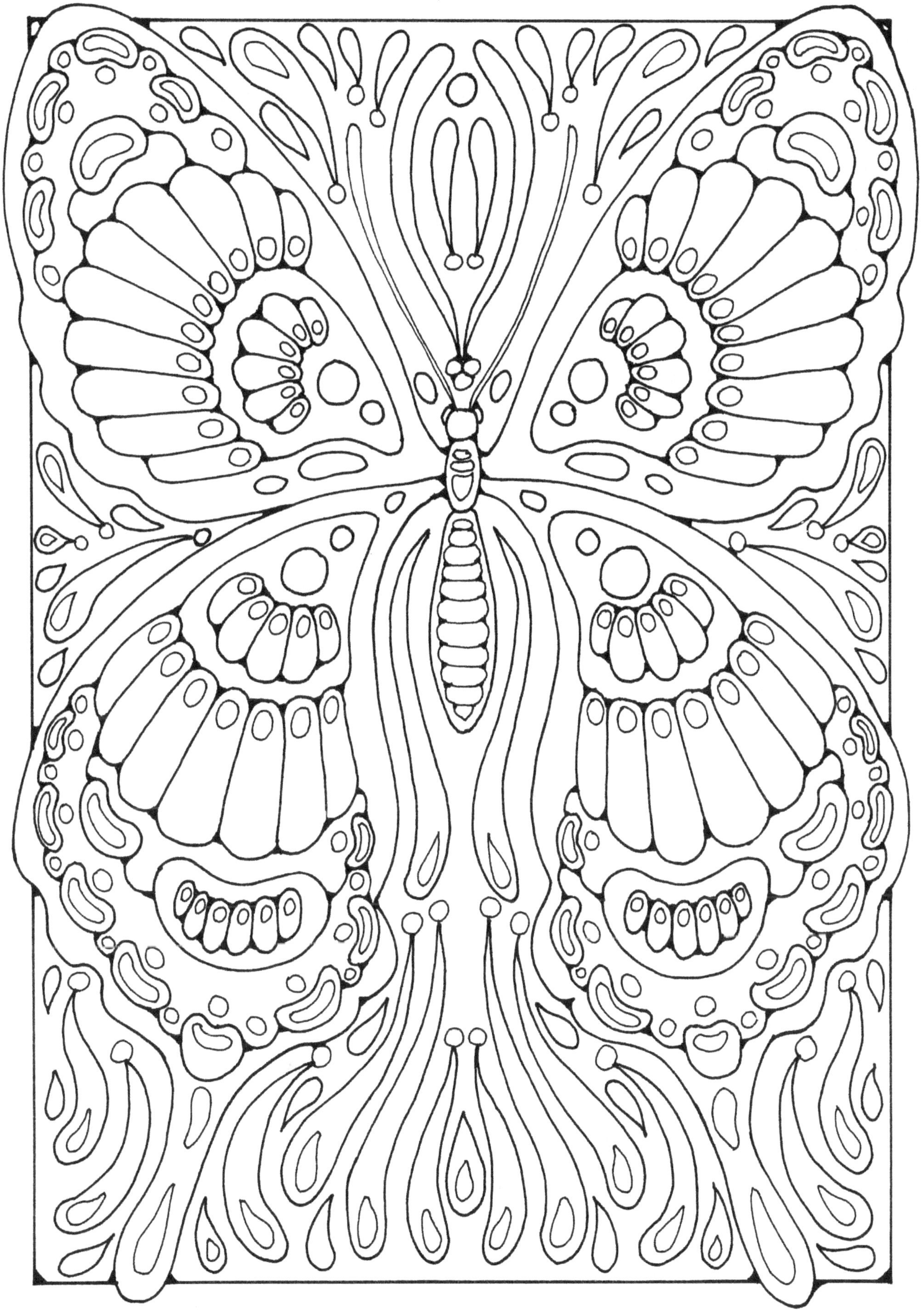

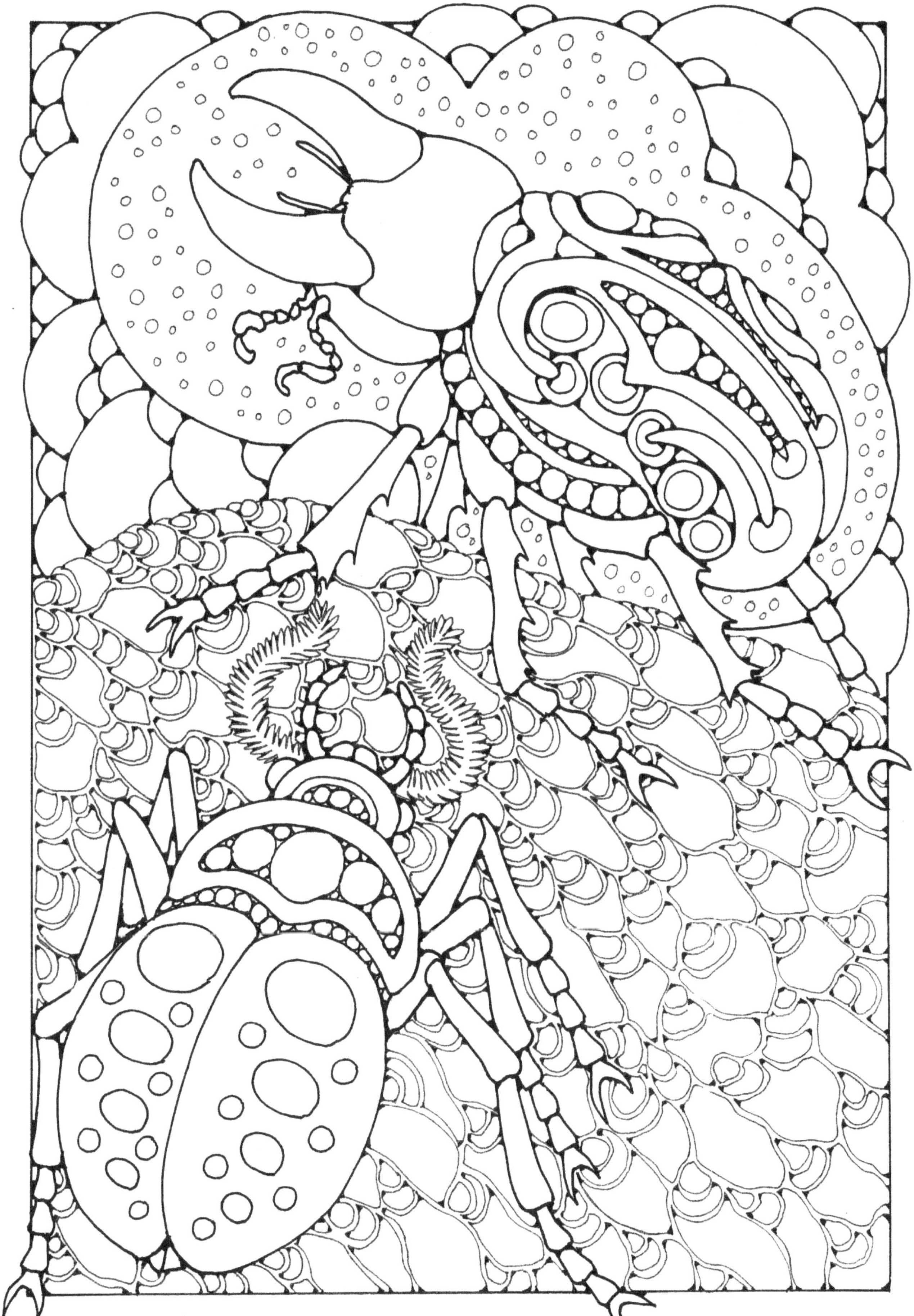

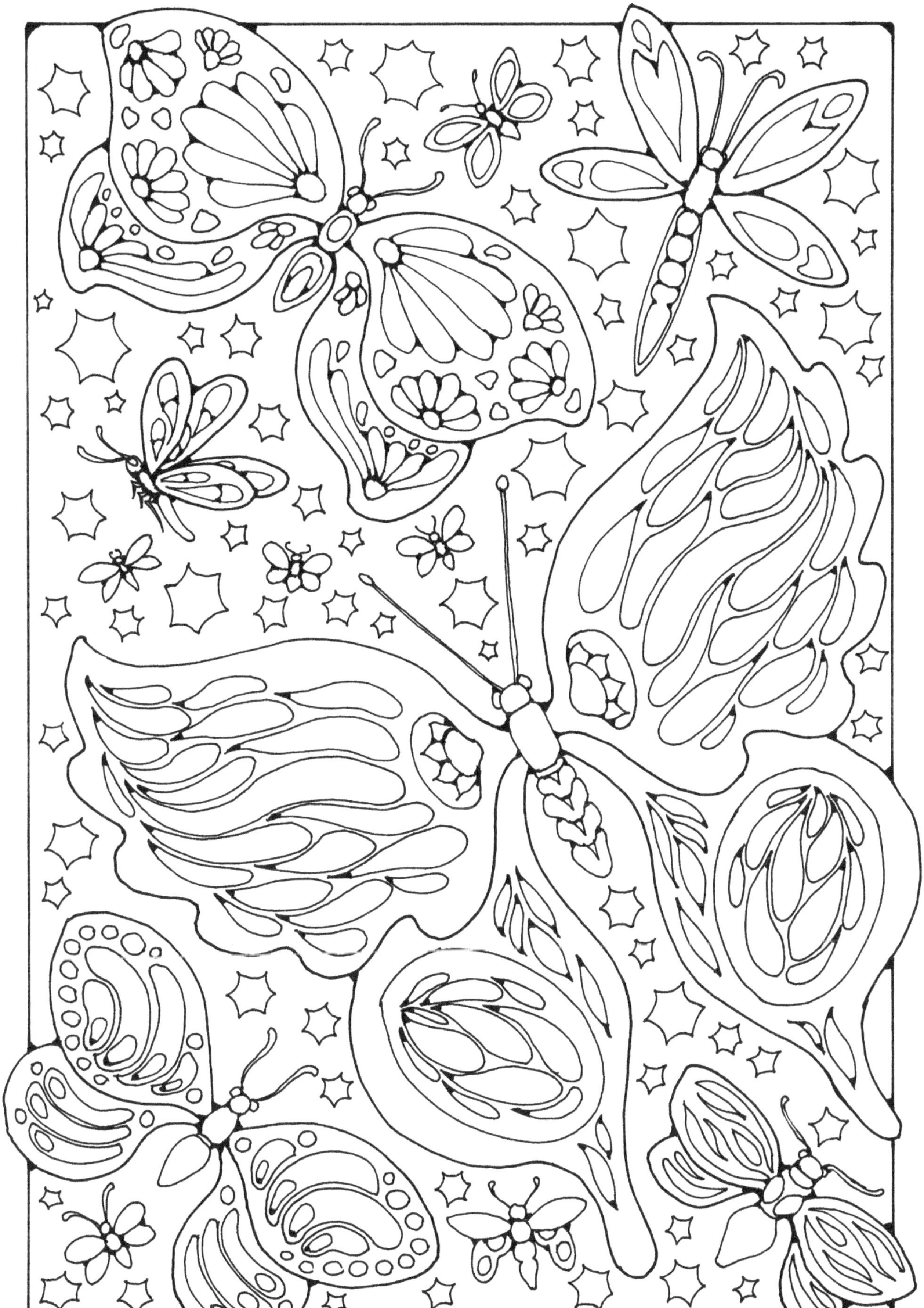

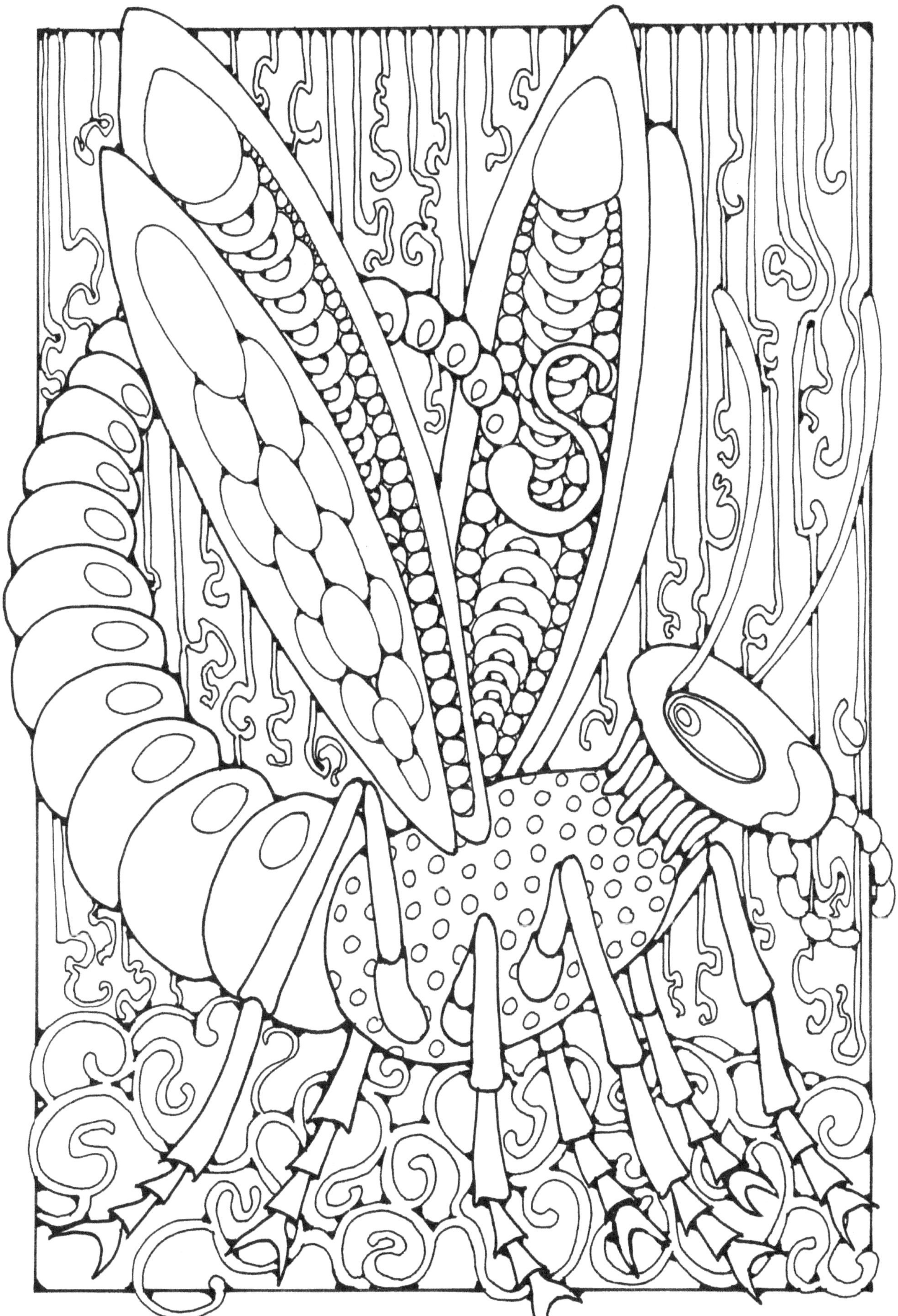

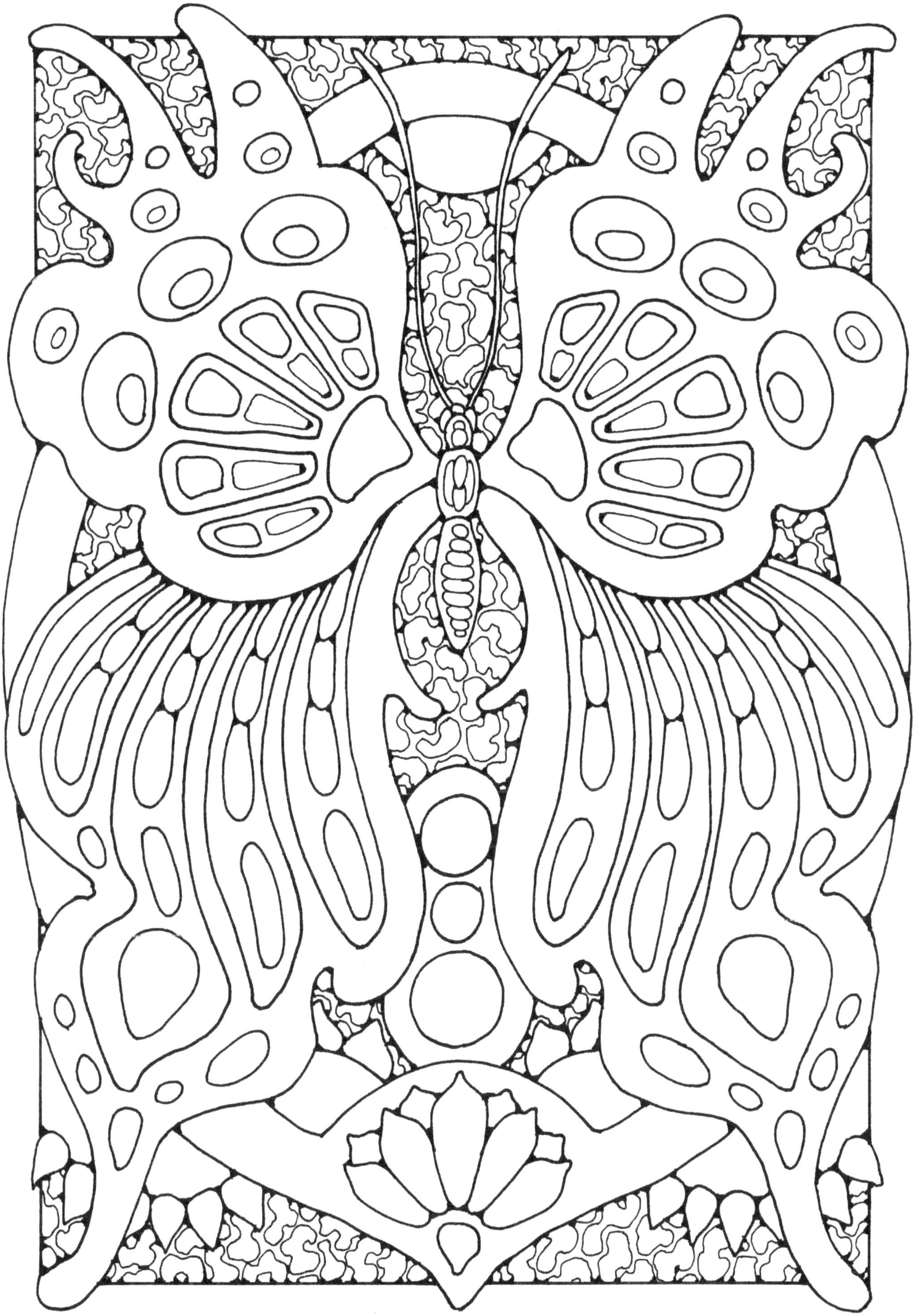

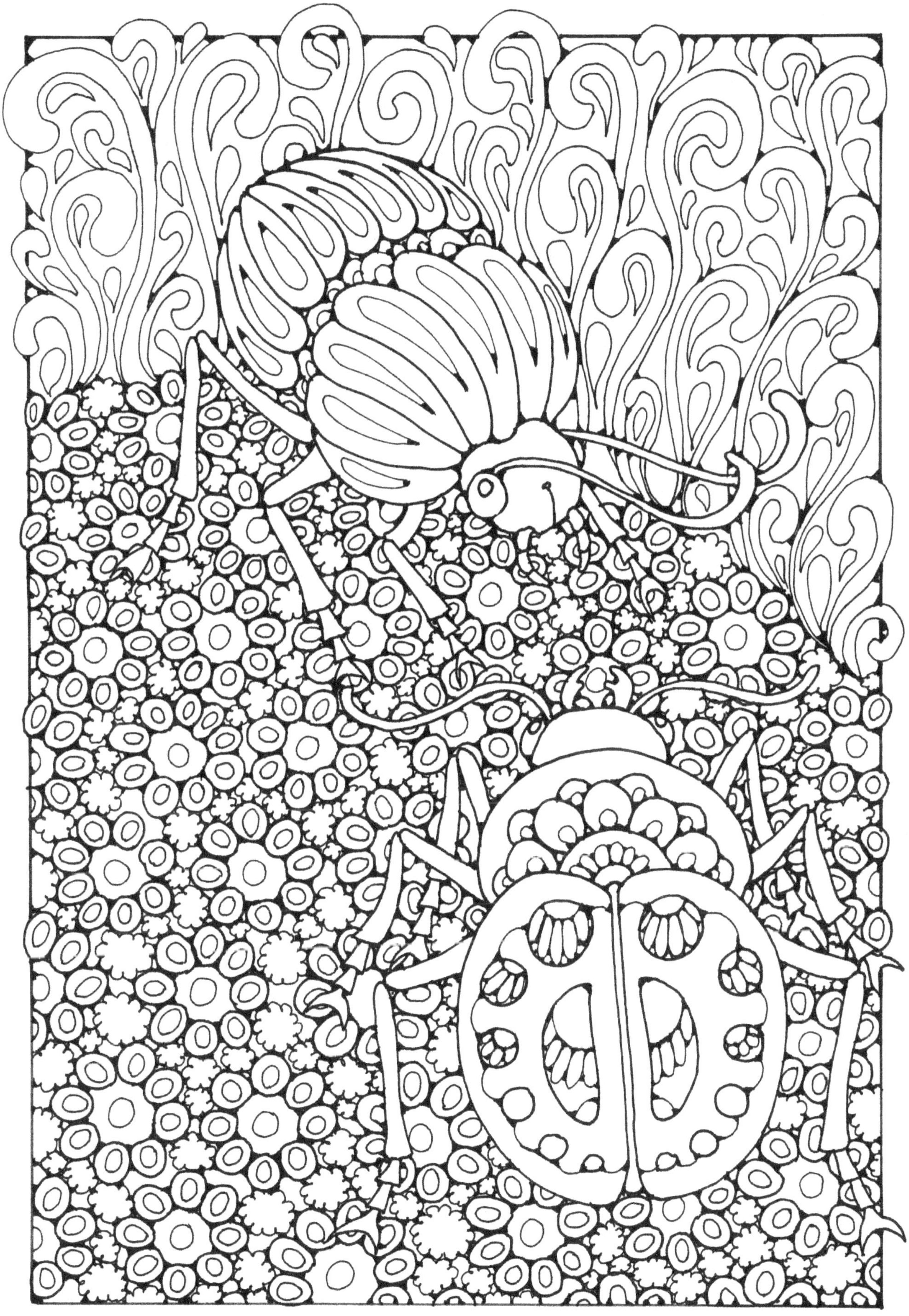

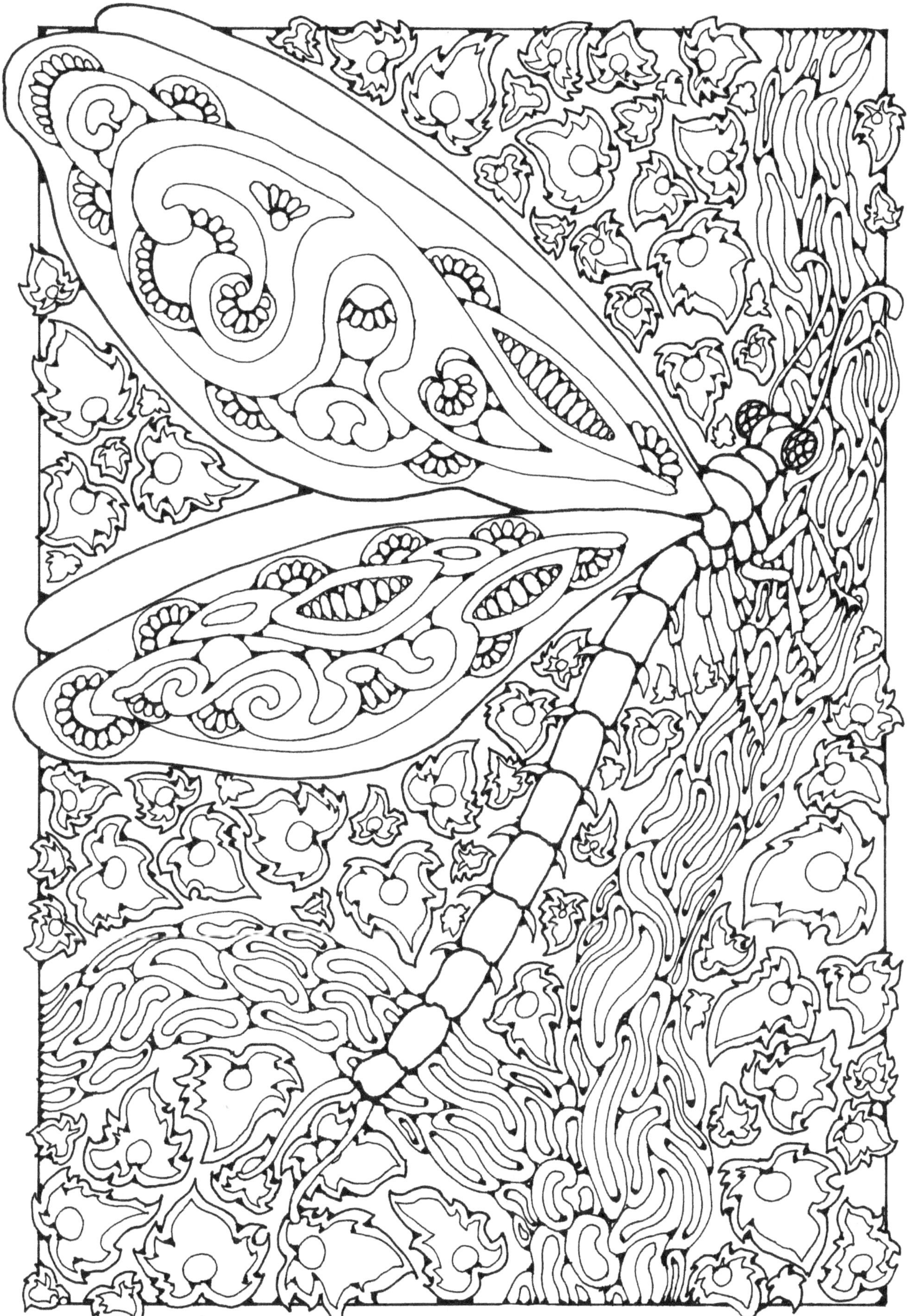

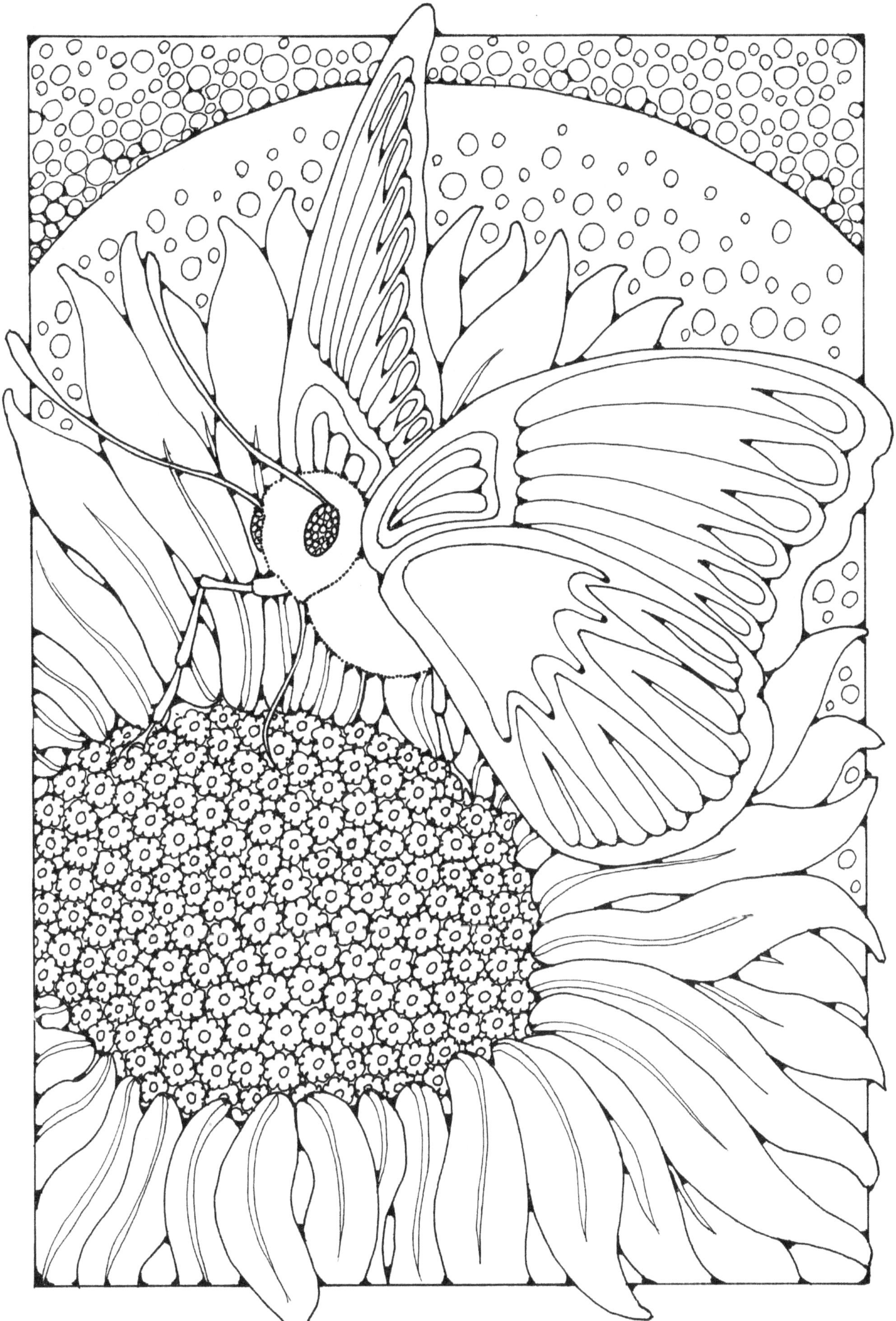

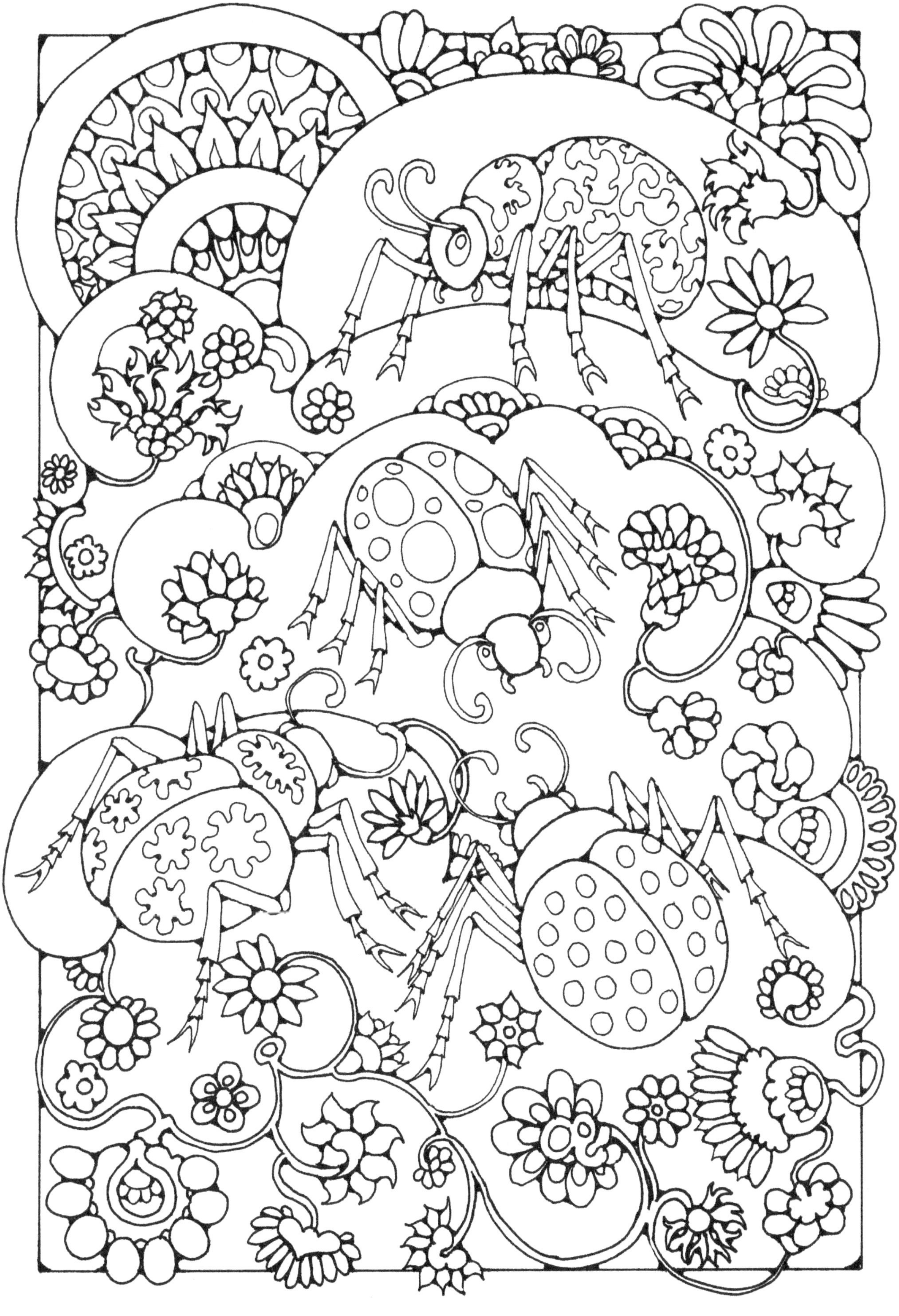

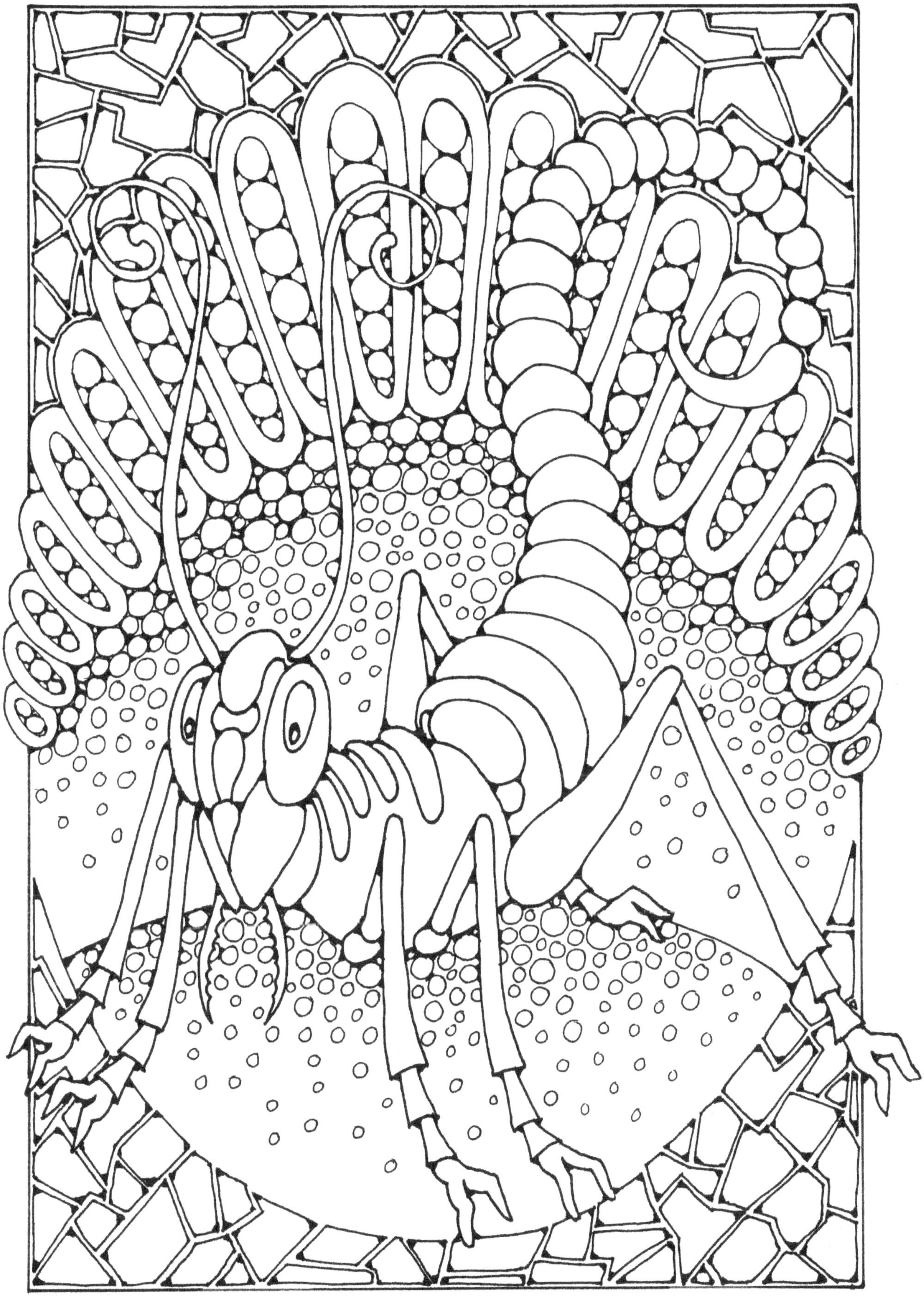

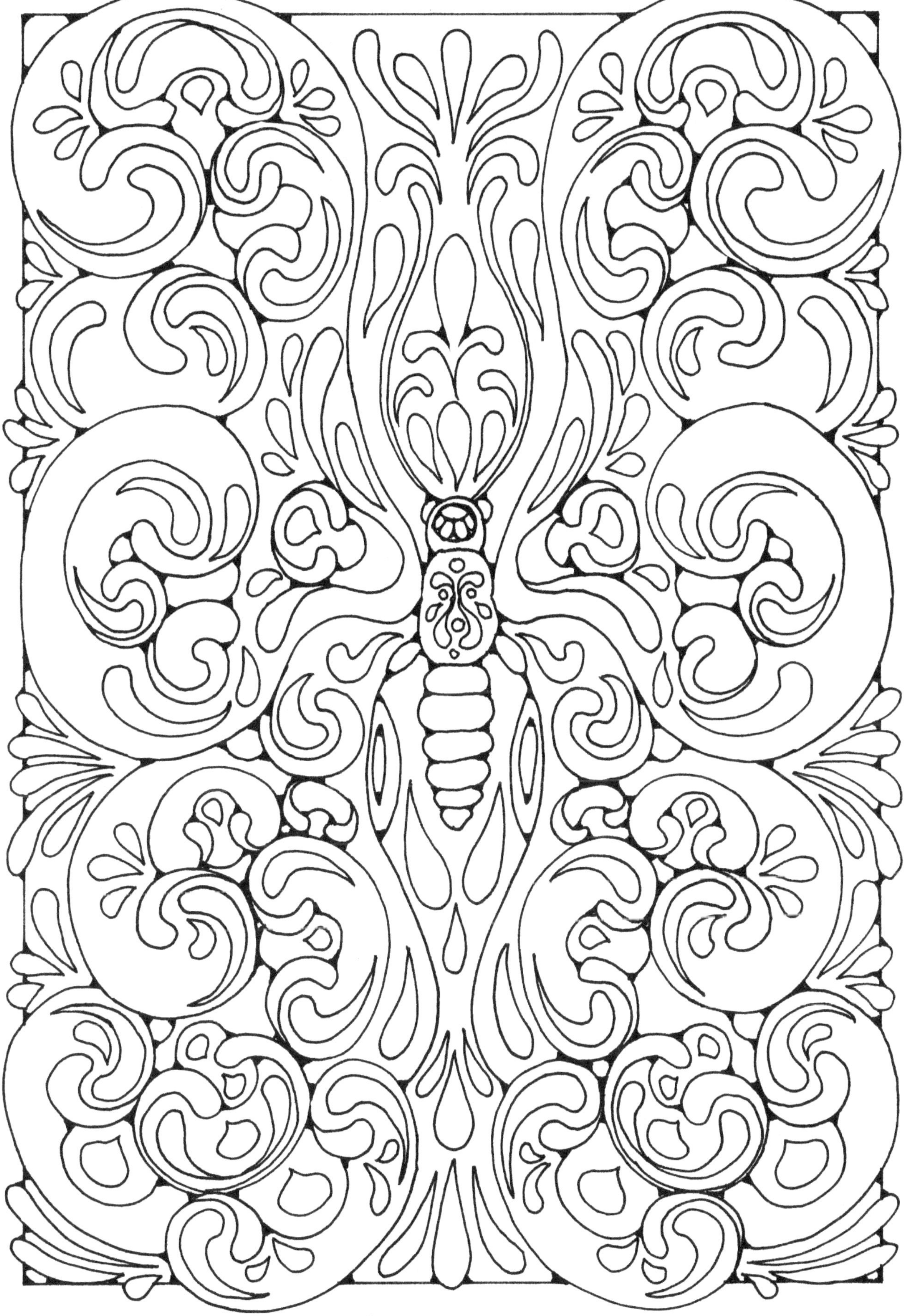

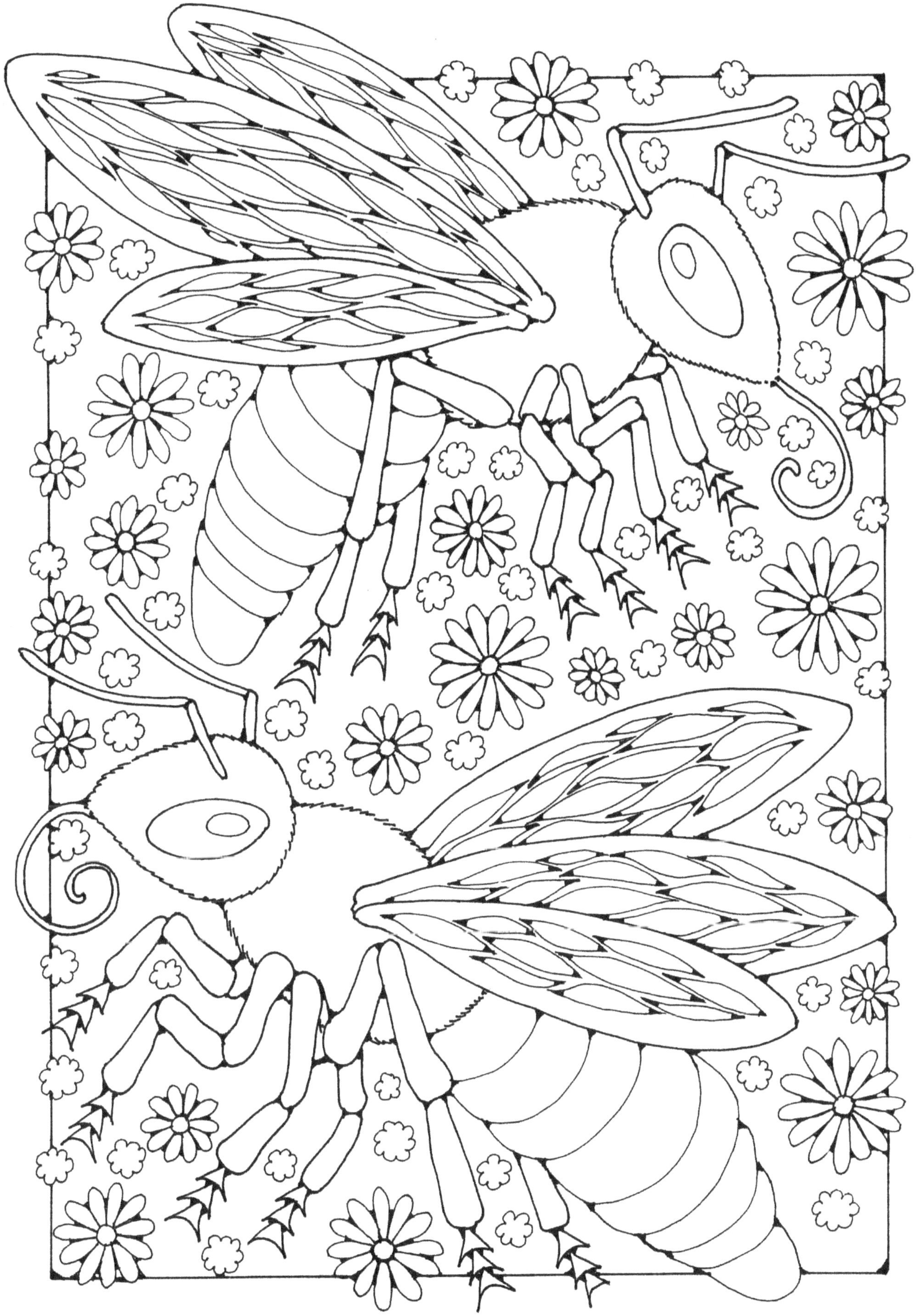

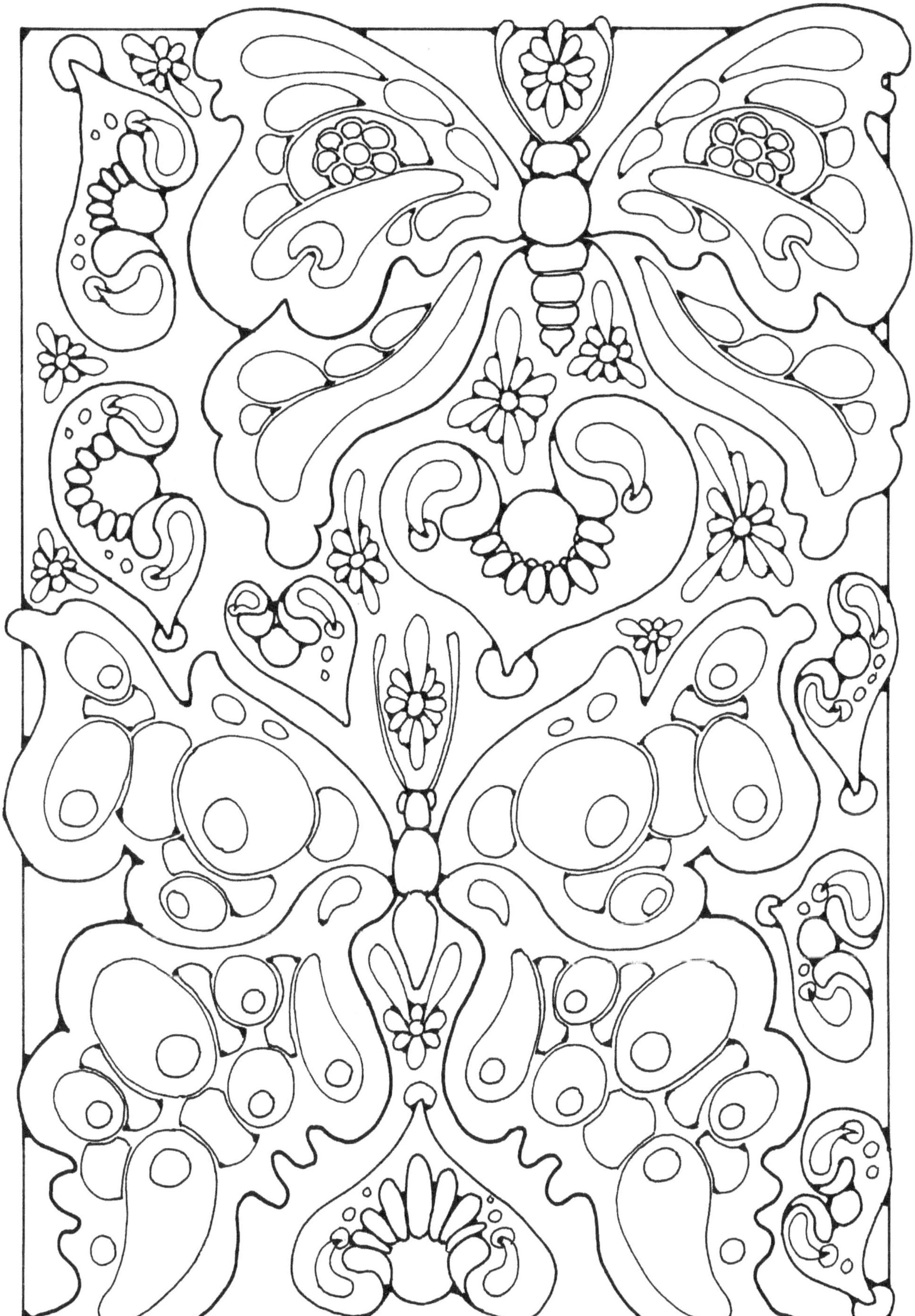

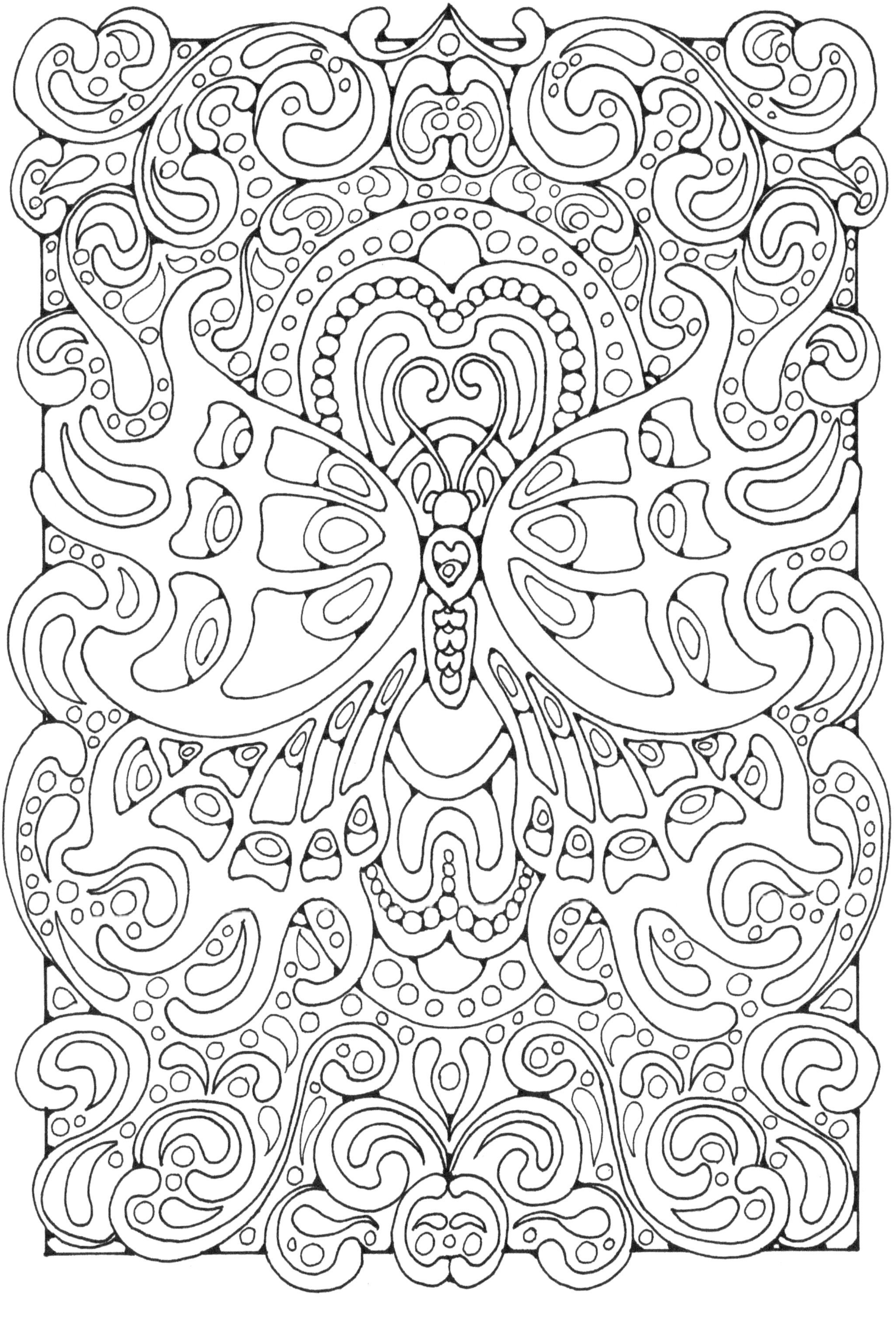

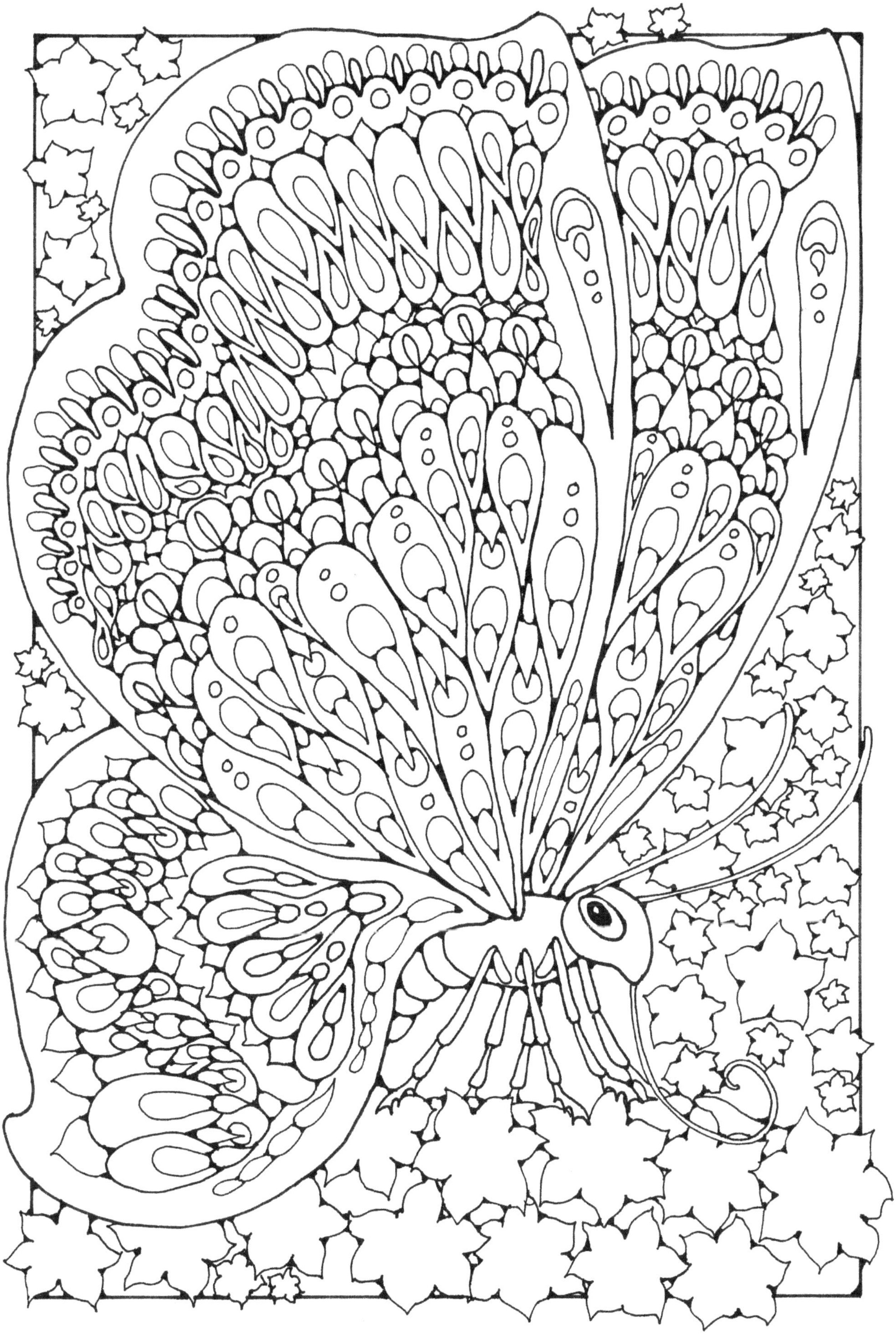

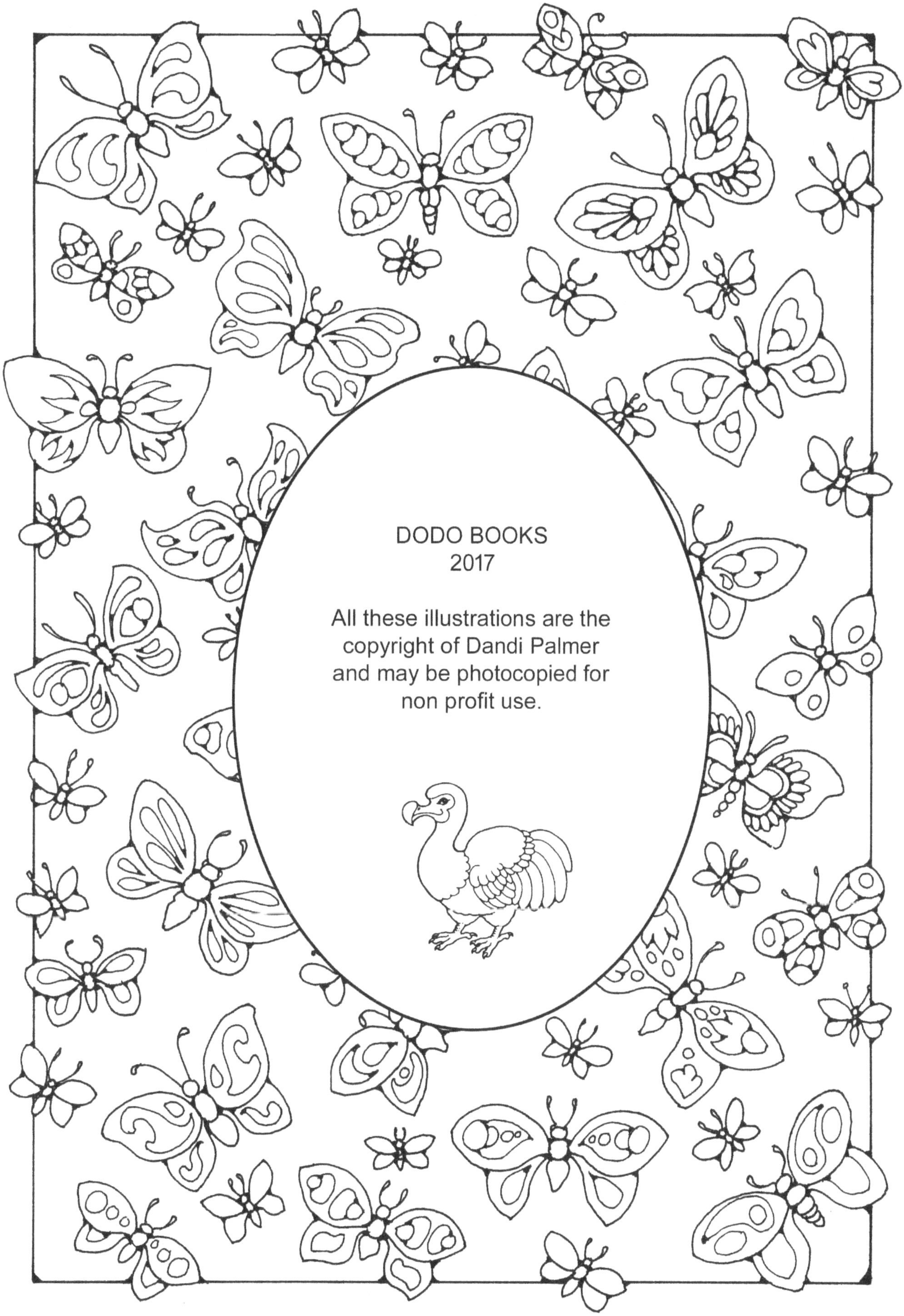

DODO BOOKS
2017

www.ingramcontent.com/pod-product-compliance
Lightning Source LLC
Chambersburg PA
CBHW081741220526
45468CB00008B/2194
* 9 7 8 1 9 0 6 4 4 2 4 9 1 *